Readers Guide
to
Intermediate
Japanese

Readers Guide

to

Intermediate

Japanese

A Quick Reference to
Written Expressions

Yasuko Ito Watt and Richard Rubinger

University of Hawai'i Press

HONOLULU

98 99 00 01 02 03   5 4 3 2 1

Library of Congress Cataloging-in-Publication Data

Watt, Yasuko Ito, 1944–
    Readers guide to intermediate Japanese : a quick reference to
written expressions / by Yasuko Ito Watt and Richard Rubinger.
    p.   cm.
    ISBN 0–8248–1993–4 (alk. paper) — ISBN 0–8248–2047–9 (pbk. :
alk. paper)
    1. Japanese language—Terms and phrases.   I. Rubinger, Richard,
1943–   . II. Title.
PL685   IN PROCESS
495.6′82421—dc21   97–41208
                                                                        CIP

Camera-ready copy prepared by the authors.

CONTENTS

ACKNOWLEDGMENTS

We are grateful to many people for their help in the preparation of this book. Anonymous readers for University of Hawai'i Press made many constructive suggestions. Professor Timothy Vance made extensive improvements in an early draft for which we are indebted. Professor Jurgis Elisonas put some life into the example sentences. Professors Kōichi Miura, Edith Sarra, and Natsuko Tsujimura made helpful comments. Professors Akiko Kakutani and Junko Suzuki provided guidance for the appendixes. Despite all the expert help we have had, errors will inevitably remain. These are, of course, the responsibility of the authors alone.

Technical help from Oda Hiromi and Sara Langer, graduate students at Indiana University, was indispensable. For financial assistance we wish to thank the Department of East Asian Languages and Cultures at Indiana University. Finally, we wish to extend our gratitude to all of our students over the years who have puzzled over complexities in written Japanese and asked the questions this book was written to answer.

INTRODUCTION

The goal of this book is to help students who are learning to read Japanese. We do not mean learning to read conversational Japanese written in Japanese script, however. Rather, our objective is to make it easier to understand texts that are written in Japanese and intended to be read. In recent years considerable attention has been given to improving the teaching of spoken Japanese. The movement for "communicative competence" has made great strides in pedagogical practice in the development of oral/aural skills. It seems to us, however, that students who seek to advance in their studies of the language to the point of doing research in Japanese sources have not been similarly supported by advances in pedagogical practice. Supplementary materials that would aid in the difficult process of attaining functional competence in written Japanese remain scarce. This book seeks to address that need.

Some excellent grammatical dictionaries have appeared in recent years, including the two volumes by Seiichi Makino and Michio Tsutsui, *A Dictionary of Beginning Japanese Grammar* (The Japan Times, 1986) and *A Dictionary of Intermediate Japanese Grammar* (The Japan Times, 1995). The present work differs from them in several important respects. This book specifically targets problems in written Japanese. We have avoided entries that we considered to be elementary and conversational, those typically covered during the first two years of most university programs. Thus, many entries found in the Makino and Tsutsui volumes are not included here, but many not included there can be found in this book. Unlike the Makino and Tsutsui volumes, ours is not intended to be a full grammatical reference. Consequently, the grammatical explanations are shorter here. We highly recommend reading Makino and Tsutsui for general review and for fuller discussions of those few entries that may appear in both. This book is addressed to students learning to read Japanese, typically in the third or fourth year of university courses, and to those who already have some facility but need a handy reference for complicated structures that they may have forgotten. Since entries are not tied to any particular textbook, a reader need not be enrolled in a formal course of study to benefit.

Entries were selected on the basis of the two authors' accumulated experience in teaching intermediate reading courses, an aggregate of some forty years. We have undertaken no systematic analysis of how often particular forms appear in written Japanese, nor have we done a systematic error analysis of learners' writing samples. We have included entries that, in our experience, students seem to have difficulty learning and remembering.

We have placed emphasis on items that cannot easily be found in the indexes of textbooks or in conventional dictionaries, either because the items are not included at all or because one cannot figure out how to look them up. Verb endings are a good example of the latter. We have included many verb endings that cause trouble for students, such as *-zaru o enai*, for example. We have not neglected patterns such as *koto ni suru/naru* or *yō ni suru/naru*, which appear frequently in written Japanese and cause difficulty because they are not readily accessible in standard reference works.

We have included many cross-references to ensure that entries lacking a standard dictionary citation form can be located easily. In some cases an idiom is entered under a particle, a practice we followed when we determined that the particle was a grammatically determining factor. Thus, *ni oite* and *ni kakete* are listed under the particle *ni* because the focus is on the idioms rather than on the gerund form of the verbs. In such cases, however, we have also included cross-references from *oite* and *kakete*, where students might also be tempted to look. Ease of access is another area in which we believe this book marks an improvement over other grammatical dictionaries. We hope that the numerous cross-references will alleviate problems caused by multiple possibilities in listing Japanese phrases and idioms that make standard references so inadequate for students.

The format for entries, with the exception of those in the appendixes, is as follows. All entries are listed in alphabetical order in romanization followed by the entry in Japanese script. The romanization is the so-called modified Hepburn system used in Kenkyūsha, Sanseidō, and other standard Japanese-English dictionaries. Where Chinese characters exist but are not commonly used, we have supplied them in brackets. Parentheses indicate a word or words that have optional usage. Cross-references appear in bold type on the same horizontal line as the entry and indicate an alternate entry listed elsewhere in the book. Except for these cross-references, the entry line is followed by a box consisting of English renderings (where appropriate), Japanese synonyms (where possible), and brief comments on structure. Finally, there are example sentences meant to illustrate how the entry is used in context. A full entry looks like this:

Entry in romanization   **entry in Japanese script**   **cross-reference**

> English rendering (where appropriate)
> Similar to: Japanese synonyms (where possible)
>
> Structure
> Structural notes
>
> See also: **Additional references**

Example sentences

We have not always provided English renderings where we felt they could be misleading or where usage in a full sentence provided a more accurate indication of meaning than a simple translation. Beneath the

English renderings (following "Similar to:") we give in italics simple Japanese synonyms, if any, that readers could be expected to know after two years' study of Japanese. The idea here is to provide meanings of more complicated expressions in terms a reader might already know, thus enhancing his or her vocabulary in the language.

In describing the structure of an entry we have provided a simple grammatical paradigm that we have found to be pedagogically useful. This is followed by an English description and further comments on structure. The paradigm consists of a shorthand where the capital letter "V" indicates verbs; the capital letter "N" indicates ordinary nouns, pronouns, *na*-nominals, and noun phrases. The capital letter "X" (and occasionally "Y" and "Z") indicates all other parts of speech and entire sentences. In the case of verbs, wherever possible we have specified the past (V-*ta*), the stem (V-stem), and the gerund form (V-*te*). V alone indicates the citation form of the verb or its negative.

Additional references following "See also:" are words or expressions related to the main entry (not necessarily exact synonyms) that might also be useful to the reader. The bold type indicates that they are listed elsewhere in the dictionary.

The example sentences are original. Recognizing that readers will have diverse skills, we have provided both simple sentences and more difficult examples that will challenge more advanced readers. All sentences are in written style, and the level of difficulty has been keyed to intermediate-level students, recognizing that this covers broad ground and a range of skills. We hope that reading some of the more difficult sentences will increase students' reading skills. In this connection please note that wherever possible we have included in the example sentences for one entry illustrations of the usages described in other entries. We have found such multiple reinforcing to be essential in the mastery of written forms at the intermediate level.

In the example sentences, readings of Chinese characters are provided in *furigana* for all but the simplest characters, and English renderings are provided as well. In the translations we have tried to walk the delicate line between acceptable English and renderings into English that will aid in understanding the structure of the Japanese original. Where that line was especially difficult to toe, we have provided an alternative translation in parentheses.

In addition to the entries in the alphabetical sections, we have added appendixes for idioms using *mi*(身) and *ki*(気). We have found these to be particularly troublesome for students. They are difficult to locate in standard reference works, as they are often embedded in brief entries that fail to include all the necessary permutations.

We no doubt have left out entries that ought to be included in this book and are guilty of other errors of omission and commission. We would appreciate comments and suggestions from readers that will aid us in compiling a better, revised edition in the future.

A

ageku (no hate) (ni) あげく（の果て）（に）

> finally; in the end; to make matters worse
>
> V-*ta ageku (no hate) (ni)*
> N *no ageku (no hate) (ni)*
> In the end, after V (and to make matters worse); in the end,
> following N (and making matters worse). *No hate ni* adds
> additional force to the statement.
> Comparable to *sue (ni)*, which also indicates an end to something
> but not necessarily an unfortunate result as with *ageku*.
>
> See also: **sue (ni)**

父は小さな会社を経営していたが、借金したあげく（の果て）（に）
破産した。

My father ran a small company, but after falling deeply into debt he
ended up going bankrupt.

彼女は長患いのあげく（の果て）（に）、幼い子供を残して夭折した。

After suffering from illness for a long time, (in the end) she died young,
leaving her little children behind.

akatsuki ni wa　あかつきには［暁には］

> in the event of; in case of
>
> V-*ta akatsuki ni wa*
> N *no akatsuki ni wa*
> In the event that V occurred; in case of N.
> Comparable to *baai ni wa*, which indicates a neutral case, but here there is the suggestion of something positive, in the sense of an event being completed with a successful outcome.

この研究が一冊の本としてめでたく出版のあかつきには、教授に昇進可能である。

In the event of this research being successfully published as a book, there is a possibility of promotion to full professor.

この計画が成功したあかつきには、お世話になった人々を食事に招待するつもりである。

If it so happens that this project is a success, I intend to invite out for a meal those who helped me.

amari (ni)　あまり（に）

> too much; excess (with positives)
>
> N *no amari (ni)*
> Too much N; an excess of N, where N is a noun expressing emotions such as "anger," "grief," or "sorrow."

私は怒りのあまり（に）、声がでなかった。

I was so angry I couldn't speak.

父は母を亡くして悲しみの<u>あまり（に）</u>、病気になってしまった。

My father was so saddened by the death of my mother that he became ill.

彼の親切に彼女は嬉しさの<u>あまり（に）</u>、涙を流して喜んだ。

She was so happy as a result of his kindness that she wept tears of joy.

aramu あらむ See **ni aran to**

aran あらん See **ni aran to**

arienai あり得ない

> not possible; cannot be
> Similar to: *zettai (ni) nai*
>
> X *wa arienai*
> Very strong negation suggesting that X is completely out of the
> question or beyond the pale.
>
> See also: **-enai; -uru; -zaru o enai**

そんな馬鹿げたことは<u>あり得ない</u>。

Such stupidity is inconceivable.

こんなに天気のいい日に雷がなるということは、絶対に<u>あり得ない</u>。

It is absolutely impossible for it to thunder on such a nice day.

ari no mama　ありのまま

> as it really is/was
>
> Used to describe unchanging situations. Can be used as a noun modifier when followed by *no* or as an adverbial expression when followed by *ni*.

父は社会的に知られた人であったが、家庭内でのありのままの姿を知っている人は少ない。

Father was (well) known in society, but there are few people who know him as he really was at home.

そのレポーターは洪水の状況をありのままに報告すべきであったにもかかわらず、創作をまじえてしたために、解雇された。

Because the correspondent included things s/he made up when s/he should have reported the conditions of the flood as they actually were, s/he was fired.

ari wa shinai　ありはしない

> out of the question; inconceivable
>
> A commonly used form of the general pattern "V-stem *wa shinai*." Similar in meaning to the negative *nai* but carries much stronger force. Often accompanied by expressions such as *nado*, *nado to iu mono/koto*, or *yō na mono/koto*, which are used in giving examples that are hard to imagine.
>
> See also: **wa shinai**

この学校はお金がないから、コンピューターなどありはしない。

This school has no money, so anything like computers is out of the question.

4

うちの校長はワンマンで、みんなで相談してものを決めるなどと
いうことは<u>ありはしない</u>。

Our principal is a one-person show, so the idea of his/her making
decisions after having consulted everyone is inconceivable.

ariyō ga nai　ありようがない

> not possible; just can't be; no way
>
> Very emphatic expression. Similar to *arienai* above.

あんなに頭のいい山本さんが、試験に失敗するなどということは
<u>ありようがない</u>。

There is absolutely no way that someone as bright as Yamamoto would
do something like fail an exam.

田中さんのような外国嫌いがヨーロッパへ行くなどということは
絶対に<u>ありようがない</u>。

It is inconceivable that a xenophobe like Tanaka would do anything like
go to Europe.

arō　あろう　See to (mo) arō

arō to suru　あろうとする　See de arō to suru; ō; ō to suru (1)

arui wa　あるいは［或いは］

(1)

> or; alternatively
> Similar to: *mata wa; ya*
>
> X *arui wa* Y, where X and Y are nouns or noun phrases.
> X or Y; X, alternatively Y.
> Another form, where *arui wa* comes at the beginning of a sentence,
> is also possible.
> X. *Arui wa* Y.

犬、あるいは猫にアレルギーの人が増えているそうだ。

It is reported that (the number of) people who are allergic to dogs or cats has been increasing.

日本史、あるいは日本文学を研究するためには、やはり日本に行った方がよかろう。

In order to do research on Japanese history or Japanese literature, it is undoubtedly better to go to Japan.

(2)

> perhaps; probably
>
> (X *wa*) *arui wa* Y
> X is probably/perhaps Y. The topic of the sentence may be
> understood from the discourse and thus is not obligatory.
> *Arui wa* indicates a degree of uncertainty.

その裁判はあるいはもう判決が出ているのかもしれない。

The judgment in that case has probably already been delivered.

ジャクソンさんはあるいはもう就職先が決まっているのではなかろうか。

Jackson has probably already decided where s/he is going to work.

6

arumai ka　あるまいか See **de wa arumai ka**

aru ni wa aru　あるにはある

> Strictly speaking such and such is the case, but . . .
>
> A commonly used form of the general pattern "V-citation form *ni wa* V-citation form," as in *iru ni wa iru* or *hanasu ni wa hanasu*, etc. While the initial statement may be true, the writer wishes to back off or qualify the statement with what follows.
>
> See also: **koto wa**

シカゴにも日本料理屋があるにはあるが、やはりニューヨークの
方が圧倒的に数が多い。

To be sure, there are Japanese restaurants in Chicago, but there are many more in New York.

中国に行ったことはあるにはあるが、今から三十年も前のことだ。

While it is true that I have been to China, that was as long as thirty years ago.

-asaru　-あさる[-漁る]

> exhaustively; extensively; voraciously
>
> V-stem-*asaru*
> The action expressed by V-stem is carried out extensively as in *tabe-asaru* (keep on eating, go around eating everywhere) or *kiki-asaru* (go everywhere and ask).

彼女は学生時代日本文学についての本を読みあさったものだ。

She used to read books on Japanese literature voraciously when she was a student.

外国語はテープを聴き<u>あさって</u>勉強することにしている。

I make it a rule to study a foreign language by listening to tapes exhaustively.

atari　あたり　See　ni atari

atte　あって　See　ni atte

-au　-合う

> V-stem-*au*
> The verb *au* added to the stem of other verbs suggests that two or more people are engaged in some reciprocal action or activity.

彼らは手紙を出し<u>合った</u>。

They sent letters to each other.

この会社のバレーボールの選手は試合の前に必ず輪になって励ま<u>し合う</u>。

This company's volleyball players always form a huddle before a game and encourage each other.

-awaseru　-合わせる

> V-stem-*awaseru*
> Happen to do V; do V without prior planning.

今朝、山田さんと通勤電車に乗り<u>合わせ</u>、おしゃべりをした。

This morning I happened to get on the commuter train with Yamada and we chatted.

8

たまたま交通事故現場に居<u>合わせた</u>ため、保険会社の質問に答え
ねばならなかった。

Because I happened to be at the site of the accident, I had to answer the
insurance company's questions.

B

-ba -ば See **o ba**

-ba ... hodo -ば〜ほど

> the more this, the more that
>
> The basic pattern is X-*ba* X *hodo* then Y, where X can be a verb, an
> adjective, or the copula *(de areba)*. The literal meaning is if X is
> the case, the more X is the case, the greater the extent of Y. More
> loosely: the more X, the more Y.

外国語は話せ<u>ば</u>話す<u>ほど</u>上手になるものだ。

With a foreign language, the more you speak the better you get. (If you
speak it, the more you speak it, the better you get.)

車は新しけれ<u>ば</u>新しい<u>ほど</u>いい。

With cars, the newer the better. (If it is new, to the extent that it is new,
it is good.)

9

田中さんは自分勝手な人なので、彼女と話をすれ<u>ば</u>する<u>ほど</u>腹が

たってくる。

Because Tanaka is such a selfish person, the more I talk with her, the angrier I get.

bakari　ばかり

(1) | just; just now
　　|
　　| V-*ta bakari*
　　| Used to express events or occurrences that have just happened.

今、着いた<u>ばかり</u>です。

I arrived just now.

彼は大学を出た<u>ばかり</u>だ。

He just graduated from college.

(2) | only
　　| Similar to: *dake*

鈴木さんは痩せたいから、サラダ<u>ばかり</u>食べている。

Because Suzuki wants to lose weight, all s/he eats is salad.

山本さんはいつ会っても子供のこと<u>ばかり</u>しか話すことがないよ

うだ。

Whenever I meet Yamamoto, all s/he seems to talk about is her/his children.

bakari de naku　ばかりでなく

> X *bakari de naku* Y
> Not just X but also Y; in addition to X there is also Y.
>
> See also: **bakari ka; ni kagirazu; ni todomarazu; nominarazu**

ロバーツさんは、スポーツがよく出来るばかりでなく、成績も
非常にいい。

Roberts is not just good at sports, s/he also gets very good grades.

コーラは、アメリカばかりでなく、世界中どこででも手に入る。

You can get Coca-Cola anywhere in the world, not just in America.

bakari ka　ばかりか

> not only . . . but also
>
> X *bakari ka* Y
> Indicates something that is not limited to X but also extends to Y.
> X is usually more to be expected or assumed to be the more normal
> element of the two.
>
> See also: **bakari de naku; ni kagirazu; ni todomarazu;
> nominarazu**

山本さんは奥さんにばかりか子供にまで馬鹿にされている。

Yamamoto is made a fool of not only by his wife (nothing unusual) but
also by his children.

小川さんは英語ばかりかフランス語もスペイン語もできる。

Ogawa can speak not only English (which, of course, everyone knows)
but also French and Spanish.

bakari ni　ばかりに

<table>
<tr><td>(1)</td><td>

because; only because; for the sole reason that
Similar to: *sore dake no riyū de*

X *bakari ni* Y
X and only X is the cause of Y.　X has an impact upon Y.

</td></tr>
</table>

彼は入学試験に合格したい<u>ばかりに</u>、健康を損ねる程、根をつめている。

All he can think of is passing the entrance exams, so he is working to the point of injuring his health.

彼女は痩せたい<u>ばかりに</u>、甘いものを全く口にしない。

All she can think of is losing weight, so she doesn't touch sweets at all.

<table>
<tr><td>(2)</td><td>

as though; as if

X *to bakari ni*
When *bakari ni* follows the particle *to*, the meaning is "as though," "as if." X can be a noun, a sentence, or a quotation.

</td></tr>
</table>

「おすしが嫌いだ」と言うと、トムは信じられない<u>とばかりに</u>、目を丸くして私の方を見た。

When I said, "I hate sushi," Tom stared at me wide-eyed as if he couldn't believe it.

高橋さんは、仕事がうまくいかなかったのは私の責任<u>とばかりに</u>、私にくってかかった。

Takahashi blamed me, as though I were responsible for his/her work not going well.

12

-bekarazaru -べからざる See -bekarazu

-bekarazu -べからず

(1)
> must not
> Similar to: V-*te wa ikenai*; V-*te wa naranai*
>
> V-*bekarazu*
> While any verb may appear in its citation form before *bekarazu*,
> with *suru* either *subekarazu* or *surubekarazu* is correct.
> *Bekarazaru* is the noun-modifying form of *bekarazu*.
>
> See also: **-beki; -beku mo nai; -beshi**

<ruby>会議中<rt>かいぎちゅう</rt></ruby>につき、この<ruby>部屋<rt>へや</rt></ruby>に<ruby>入<rt>はい</rt></ruby>る<u>べからず</u>。

A meeting is in session, so no one may enter this room.

<ruby>口<rt>くち</rt></ruby>にす<u>べからざる</u>ことを口にしてしまい<ruby>後悔<rt>こうかい</rt></ruby>している。

I regret saying things that should not have been said.

(2)
> cannot
> Similar to: *koto ga dekinai*
>
> V-*bekarazu*
> While any verb may appear in its citation form before *bekarazu*,
> with *suru* either *subekarazu* or *surubekarazu* is correct.
> *Bekarazaru* is the noun-modifying form of *bekarazu*.
>
> See also: **-beki; -beku mo nai; -beshi**

<ruby>子<rt>こ</rt></ruby>を<ruby>亡<rt>な</rt></ruby>くした<ruby>親<rt>おや</rt></ruby>の<ruby>気持<rt>きも</rt></ruby>ちは、いかんにも<ruby>描写<rt>びょうしゃ</rt></ruby>す<u>べからず</u>。

The feeling of a parent who has lost a child cannot be described in any way.

<ruby>戦争中<rt>せんそうちゅう</rt></ruby>、<ruby>想像<rt>そうぞう</rt></ruby>す<u>べからざる</u><ruby>苦<rt>くる</rt></ruby>しみを<ruby>味<rt>あじ</rt></ruby>わった。

During the war I experienced suffering of a kind that cannot be imagined.

13

-beki -べき

> must, should, supposed to
> Similar to: *-nakute wa ikenai*; *-nakute wa naranai*
>
> V-*beki*
> A form of the classical suffix *-beshi* (see below). Conveys obligation, compulsion, propriety. The noun-modifying form is *-beki* alone (with *-bekarazaru* as the corresponding negative), whereas the sentence-final form is commonly *-beki da* rather than the classical sentence-ending form *-beshi*. While any verb may appear in its citation form before *-beki*, in the case of *suru* either *su* or *suru* is correct.
>
> See also: **-bekarazu; -beku mo nai; -beshi**

子供の将来を思えば、毎日学校に行かせるべきだ。

If you are considering the child's future, you must send him/her to school every day.

大学に進むかどうかは、よく考えるべきことだ。

Whether or not to go on to college is something that should be thought over carefully.

-beku mo nai   -べくもない

> no way something can be done; can't be done even if one wanted to
> Similar to: *shiyō ni mo totemo dekinai; suru hōhō ga nai; suru yochi mo nai*
>
> V-*beku mo nai*
> In addition to strong negation, there is also a sense of resignation. Often follows verbs that indicate the writer's wish or hope, such as *nozomu* or *sōzō suru*. While any verb may be used in its citation form before *-beku mo nai*, with *suru* either *su* or *suru* is correct.
>
> See also: **-bekarazu; -beki; -beshi**

彼は、その女が自分の生みの親であるということを知る<u>べくもな</u>
<u>かった</u>。

There was no way for him to know that that woman was his natural
mother.

社長になるなど望む<u>べくもない</u>ことである。

There is no way that s/he could hope to become president of the
company.

-beshi -べし

> shall, ought to, will, be expected to
>
> Derives from a classical form and includes meanings of propriety,
> conjecture, possibility, and intention. In modern Japanese *-beki da*
> is commonly used in its place. While any verb may be used in its
> citation form before *-beshi*, with *suru* either *su* or *suru* is correct.
>
> See also: **-bekarazu; -beki; -beku mo nai**

病気にならぬよう、よく運動す<u>べし</u>。

In order not to get sick, you ought to exercise often.

明朝、会議があるので、八時までには来る<u>べし</u>。

There is a meeting tomorrow morning, so you should get here by eight.

五カ条のご誓文から

From the Five Article Charter Oath (6 April 1868)

一、広ク会議ヲ興シ万機公論ニ決ス<u>ベシ</u>

Item: An assembly shall be widely convoked and all measures
shall be decided by open discussion.

15

<ruby>一、旧来の陋習ヲ破リ天地ノ公道ニ基クベシ<rt>ひとつ きゅうらい ろうしゅう やぶ てんち こうどう もとづ</rt></ruby>

Item: Evil practices of the past shall be abandoned, and actions shall be based on international usage.

<ruby>一、知識ヲ世界ニ求メ大ニ皇基ヲ振起スベシ<rt>ひとつ ちしき せかい もと おおい こうき しんき</rt></ruby>

Item: Knowledge shall be sought throughout the world, and the foundations of imperial rule shall be strengthened.

C

chigai nai ちがいない See **ni chigai nai**

D

dake atte だけあって

> as may (might) be expected
>
> X *dake atte* Y
> Because of X one might naturally expect Y. Gives the likely reason for Y to occur. The emphasis is on Y.

彼女は日本語を二十年も教えているだけあって、どんな文法でも簡単に説明できる。

She can explain any grammar point easily, as might be expected from one who has been teaching Japanese for twenty years.

彼はオスカーをもらった<u>だけあって</u>、さすがに演技がうまい。

He is certainly a good actor, as might be expected from one who received an Oscar.

dake ni　だけに

> because; inasmuch as
>
> X *dake ni* Y
> Because of X, then Y. Suggests that Y is the natural outcome of X.
> In contrast to *dake atte* (above), the emphasis is on X. X exists and therefore Y is a natural outcome.

大統領の訪問を楽しみにしていた<u>だけに</u>、中止になって非常にがっかりした。

Because we were looking forward to the president's visit, we were very disappointed when it was canceled.

スミスさんは日本に長い間住んでいた<u>だけに</u>、日本のことに詳しい。

Inasmuch as Smith lived in Japan for a long time, s/he knows a great deal about it (as one might expect).

dake no　だけの

> be enough for; be sufficient for
>
> V *dake no* N, where V is a verb in the potential form.
> N is sufficient to enable V.

新しい仕事は、生活できる<u>だけの</u>給料がもらえるからうれしい。

I'm happy with my new job, because I get a salary that's sufficient to live on.

17

この<ruby>教室<rt>きょうしつ</rt></ruby>は小さいが、<ruby>十人<rt>じゅうにん</rt></ruby>ぐらいの学生が<ruby>座<rt>すわ</rt></ruby>れる<u>だけの</u><ruby>席<rt>せき</rt></ruby>はある。

This classroom is small, but it has enough seats for about ten students.

dake no koto wa aru　だけのことはある

> be worthwhile
>
> X *dake no koto wa aru*
> Indicates that X is worthwhile and not a waste of time.

<ruby>夏目漱石<rt>なつめそうせき</rt></ruby>の<ruby>作品<rt>さくひん</rt></ruby>は<ruby>難<rt>むずか</rt></ruby>しいが、<ruby>読<rt>よ</rt></ruby>む<u>だけのことはある</u>。

The works of Natsume Sōseki are difficult, but there is value in reading them.

その<ruby>政治家<rt>せいじか</rt></ruby>は<ruby>話<rt>はなし</rt></ruby>がうまいので、<ruby>遠<rt>とお</rt></ruby>くまで<ruby>出<rt>で</rt></ruby>かけて行って聞く<u>だけのことはある</u>。

Since that politician is a good speaker, it is worthwhile traveling a great distance just to hear her/him.

-dasu　-出す

> (1)　V-stem-*dasu*
> Begin to V; begin V-ing; start to V.
> V-stem-*dasu* and V-stem-*hajimeru* are often interchangeable.
>
> See also:　**-kakeru**

<ruby>雨<rt>あめ</rt></ruby>が<ruby>降<rt>ふ</rt></ruby>り<u>出した</u>。

It began to rain.

18

その子供は一才にならないうちに歩き<u>出</u>し、二才の時に話し<u>出</u>し、四才の時に読み<u>出した</u>。

Before s/he was one year old that child began to walk, at two s/he began to talk, and at four s/he began to read.

---

(2) V-stem-*dasu*
Used in the sense of creating or giving birth to something significant. Limited to a small number of verbs meaning "to create or produce."

日本文化は能、歌舞伎などの芸能を生み<u>出した</u>。

Japanese culture brought forth arts such as Noh and Kabuki.

彼女は廃棄物を使ってすばらしい芸術品を作り<u>出した</u>。

Using waste materials, she produced wonderful works of art.

de aran　であらん　See　**ni aran to**

de arō　であろう

---

perhaps; probably

X *de arō*
X may be the case; probably X.
Can be replaced by *darō*.

See also: **-ō (2)**

ここから大学までの距離は三十分ぐらい<u>であろう</u>。

It's probably something like thirty minutes from here to the university.

19

あの人はウィルソンさん<u>であろう</u>と思うのだが、服装^{ふくそう}がいつもと違^{ちが}っているのでウィルソンさんでないかもしれない。

I think that person is probably Wilson, but his/her attire is different from the usual, so maybe it isn't Wilson.

de arō to suru　であろうとする

> try to be; attempt to be; be on the point of
>
> N *de arō to suru*
> Try to be N.
> The copula form of the more general pattern *-ō to suru*. Originates in the classical Japanese expression *aramu to su*, which can be translated as "try to be" or "intend to be," as in the examples below.
>
> **See also: -ō (1); -ō to suru (1); ni aran to**

一国^{いっこく}のリーダー<u>であろうとする</u>者^{もの}は、公平^{こうへい}でなければならぬ。

One who would lead a nation must be impartial.

平和^{へいわ}に誠実^{せいじつ}<u>であろうとする</u>者^{もの}は、先^まず、平和が力^{ちから}の均衡^{きんこう}によって保^{たも}たれているという事実^{じじつ}を認^{みと}めなければならぬ。

Those who would be faithful to peace must first recognize the reality that peace is maintained by a balance of power.

彼女^{かのじょ}に対^{たい}していくら親切^{しんせつ}<u>であろうとして</u>も、彼女がとり合^あってくれないから話^{はなし}にならない。

No matter how much I try to be kind to her, she doesn't pick up on it, so it's not worth the effort.

20

demo　でも

> X *demo*
> Some (thing, place, one) like X. X is given as an example and is
> not insisted upon.
>
> See also: **nari (2); to demo**

お昼にそば<u>でも</u>食べようかと思う。

I'm thinking of having *soba* or something for lunch.

みんな新宿か銀座へ<u>でも</u>出かけたにちがいない。

I'm sure that everyone went off to Shinjuku or Ginza or someplace like that.

demo nan demo nai　でも何でもない

> N *demo nan demo nai*
> Nothing at all to do with N; not in any way at all N. Used for very
> strong negation.

あの人は友達<u>でも何でもない</u>。同じ授業に出ているだけである。

That person is not in any way at all a friend. S/He is only taking the
same course.

長髪がいけないというのは校則<u>でも何でもない</u>、ただあの先生が
言い出したことである。

The prohibition on long hair has nothing to do with school rules; it is
just something thought up by that teacher.

de sumasu　で済ます　See sumasu

21

de sumaseru　で済ませる　See **sumasu**

de tamaranai　でたまらない　See **tamaranai**

de wa arumai ka　ではあるまいか

> Isn't it probably the case that . . . ; Don't you think that . . . ; I
> wonder if perhaps . . .
> Similar to: *-nai darō ka; -nakarō ka*
>
> N *de wa arumai ka*
> I wonder if N; I'm afraid that N.
>
> See also: **-mai ka to**

今日はこんな大雪だから、山田さんは、来られないの<u>ではあるま
いか</u>。

Because the snowfall is so heavy today, I'm afraid that Yamada won't be
able to come.

あの人は頭が固いから、こちらの言うことを分かろうとしない。
これ以上、話しても無駄<u>ではあるまいか</u>。

That person is stubborn, so s/he makes no attempt to understand what we
say. I'm afraid it is useless to speak with her/him any more.

dokoro ka　どころか

> far from
>
> X *dokoro ka* Y
> The intention is to go beyond X and to achieve Y; far from X, Y is the case (as in the first two examples). In the negative form, the meaning is "one cannot do Y, to say nothing of X," where Y is considerably beyond X and where Y is contrary to what one might expect, as in the last two examples. Can be used for both favorable and unfavorable situations.

斉藤さんは、全然出来ないのに、勉強をやめる<u>どころか</u>、博士課程に入りたいそうだ。

Saitō just doesn't have it, but far from giving up her/his studies, I hear s/he wants to enter the doctoral program.

村上さんは、この本はつまらないと言ったが、つまらない<u>どころか</u>、とてもおもしろい。

Murakami said this book is boring but (I think that) far from being dull, it is quite interesting.

カーターさんは、和食はさしみ<u>どころか</u>、てんぷらさえも食べない。

Among Japanese foods, Carter won't even eat tempura, let alone sashimi.

ジョーンズさんはもう三年も日本語を勉強しているが、漢字<u>どころか</u>平仮名さえ、まだよく書けない。

Jones has been studying Japanese for (as long as) three years but still can't even write *hiragana* well, to say nothing of *kanji*.

domo　ども　See **to iedomo**

dore dake　どれだけ　See **ika ni (2)**

dōri　どおり　See **tōri**

E

-enai　-得ない

> unable to; cannot
> Similar to: *koto ga dekinai*
>
> V-stem-*enai*
>
> See also: **arienai; -uru; -zaru o enai**

<ruby>日米間<rt>にちべいかん</rt></ruby>の<ruby>貿易摩擦<rt>ぼうえきまさつ</rt></ruby>がいまだに<ruby>続<rt>つづ</rt></ruby>いていることは<ruby>否定<rt>ひてい</rt></ruby>し<u>得ない</u>。

We cannot deny that trade friction between the United States and Japan continues.

うちを<ruby>出<rt>で</rt></ruby>るということを<ruby>母<rt>はは</rt></ruby>に<ruby>言<rt>い</rt></ruby>い<ruby>出<rt>だ</rt></ruby>し<u>得なかった</u>。

I couldn't bring myself to tell my mother that I was leaving home.

-eru　-得る　See **-uru**

F

fujiyū suru 不自由する See **ni fujiyū suru**

fū ni 風に See **to iu fū ni**

G

-gachi がち

> be apt to; liable to; prone to
>
> X-*gachi*, where X is a noun or a verb stem.
> Expresses a tendency to X.

<ruby>山本<rt>やまもと</rt></ruby>さんは<ruby>出張<rt>しゅっちょう</rt></ruby>が<ruby>多<rt>おお</rt></ruby>いから、いつも<ruby>留守<rt>るす</rt></ruby>がちである。

Yamamoto often goes away on business trips, so he is apt to be away from home all the time.

<ruby>選挙演説<rt>せんきょえんぜつ</rt></ruby>の時に<ruby>約束<rt>やくそく</rt></ruby>したことを<ruby>忘<rt>わす</rt></ruby>れてしまうのは、<ruby>政治家<rt>せいじか</rt></ruby>にありがちのことである。

Forgetting promises made in campaign speeches is something politicians are prone to do.

ga hayai ka　が早いか

> as soon as; no sooner than; the moment that
>
> V *ga hayai ka* X
> X occurs immediately after V; or, as soon as V then X.
>
> See also: **ka to miru to; nari (1); soba kara; totan (ni); ya ina ya**

文子は夫の母がやって来ると聞くが早いか、家の片付けを始めた。

The moment she heard that her husband's mother was coming, Fumiko started straightening up the house.

動物にアレルギーのトムは、猫のすがたをみるが早いか、くしゃみを始めた。

Tom, who is allergic to animals, began to sneeze the moment he saw a cat.

ga yue ni　が故に　See **yue ni**

gotoku　如く

> like, in the manner of
> Similar to: *yō ni*
>
> X (*no*) *gotoku*, where *no* is used when X is a noun.
> In the manner of X; similar to X.

日本の自動車産業は、上述の如く、外国に工場を設置する方向に進んで行った。

As stated above, the Japanese automobile industry has moved ahead toward establishing factories in foreign countries.

26

戦争の成り行きは国民の憂慮した<u>如く</u>、徐々に悪化して行ったの
であった。

Just as the people feared, the course of the war gradually worsened.

gurai　ぐらい　See kurai

gyaku ni ieba　逆にいえば　See gyaku ni iu to

gyaku ni iu to　逆にいうと

---

conversely; to turn things around; to put it differently

X. *Gyaku ni iu to* Y.
Y reverses the perspective of X.

日本経済はアメリカに大きな市場をもっている。<u>逆にいうと</u>アメ
リカは日本製品に依存しているということである。

The Japanese economy has a large market in America. Put another way,
America is dependent on Japanese products.

東京は密集した近代都市で、どこもここも建物だらけである。<u>逆
にいうと</u>緑が少ないということである。

Tokyo is a congested modern metropolis. It is filled with buildings
everywhere. Conversely, it has little greenery.

H

habakaranai はばからない

> unhesitating; unafraid; not shy; forthright; without compunction
>
> V-*te habakaranai*
> Does not hesitate to V even when restraint might be called for.
>
> See also: **habakaru tokoro naku**

彼は自分がクラスで一番よく出来る学生だと言って<u>はばからな</u>
<u>かった</u>。

He had no compunction about saying that he was the best student in the
class.

私は誰の前であろうと、自分の意見を述べて<u>はばからない</u>つもりだ。
I intend to be forthright in expressing my views in front of anyone.

habakaranai de はばからないで See **habakaru tokoro naku**

habakarazu はばからず See **habakaru tokoro naku**

habakaru tokoro naku　はばかるところなく

> without hesitating; openly; without regret
> Similar to: *ki ni shinai de*
>
> One does not hesitate even in circumstances where the result might not be favorable.
>
> See also: **habakaranai**

彼は英語の発音が非常に悪いにもかかわらず、<u>はばかるところなく</u>、あらゆる所へ出かけて行って英語で日本についての話をする。

Although his English pronunciation is very bad, he goes all over and without hesitation gives talks about Japan in English.

彼女は<u>はばかるところなく</u>、運動靴をはいて一流のレストランへ出かけて行く。

She goes out to first-class restaurants in her running shoes without a thought.

hajimete　はじめて　See **ni shite hajimete; -te hajimete**

hatashite　果たして

> (1) 　sure enough; as expected; indeed
> Similar to: *omotte ita tōri*; *yahari*
>
> Confirms one's expectations.

彼は日本に大地震が起こると言っていたが、<u>果たして</u>本当になってしまった。

He was saying that there would be a big earthquake in Japan, and indeed there was.

---

(2) | really; actually; in fact
Similar to: *hontō ni*; *ittai*

現総理大臣の辞職が<u>果たして</u>事実とすれば、後継者は誰であろうか。

If in fact the current prime minister is going to resign, who do you suppose will be his/her successor?

円が急激に高くなっているということは<u>果たして</u>どんなことを意味するのであろうか。

What on earth is the meaning of the sudden rise in (the value of) the yen?

hayai ka　早いか　See **ga hayai ka**

hazu ga nai　はずがない

---

no expectation; cannot be the case

X *(no) hazu ga nai*, where *no* is used when X is a noun.
There is no expectation that X is the case.

あんなにホットドッグの好きな高橋さんが菜食主義者の<u>はずがない</u>。

Takahashi, who loves hot dogs so much, surely is not a vegetarian.

30

映画通の山本さんが先月封切りされたフランス映画をまだ見てい

ないはずがない。

It is certain that Yamamoto, an authority on film, has already seen the
French movie that opened last month. (There's no expectation that s/he
hasn't seen it yet.)

hodo　ほど

> extent; degree
>
> X *hodo*
> The degree or extent of X.
>
> See also: **kurai**

杉村さんは非常に頭のいい人である。天才と言ってもいいほどである。

Sugimura is so smart that we could almost say s/he is a genius.

秋の空ほど変わりやすいものはないとはよく言われることである。

It is often said that there is nothing as changeable as the autumn sky.

hodo de wa nai　ほどではない　See　**hodo wa nai**

hodo no　ほどの　See　**(to iu) hodo no . . . nai**

hodo wa nai　ほどはない

> not to the extent or degree of
>
> X *wa* Y *hodo wa nai*, where X and Y are nouns.
> X is not to the extent or degree of Y.

この山の高さは富士山<u>ほどはない</u>。

This mountain is not as high as Mt. Fuji. (The height of this mountain is not as great as that of Mt. Fuji.)

木村さんの学力は吉田さん<u>ほどはない</u>。

Kimura's academic talent does not measure up to Yoshida's.

hoka nai　ほかない　See (yori) hoka (ni) shikata ga nai; (yori) hoka (wa) nai

hoka naranai　ほかならない

> nothing but; nothing other than
>
> X *wa* Y *ni hoka naranai*
> X is nothing other than Y. Negates all other possibilities.

あんなに元気だった内田さんが病気になったのは、無理をし過ぎたからに<u>ほかならない</u>。

The reason a person as healthy as Uchida got sick can't be anything but overwork.

あの人の考えは個人主義ではなく、利己主義に<u>ほかならない</u>。

That person's ideas do not represent individualism; they are nothing other than egoism.

hoka naranu ほかならぬ See **hoka naranai**

hoka (ni) michi wa nai ほか（に）途はない See **(yori) hoka (ni) michi ga nai**

hoka (ni) shikata ga nai ほか（に）仕方がない See **(yori) hoka (ni) shikata ga nai**

hoshii 欲しい See **-te hoshii**

I

ichiō 一応

---

for the time being; for now

Used to introduce a point or statement that is temporary or provisional rather than firm or complete.

詳細は後述することにして、<u>一応</u>概要を述べておく。

The details we will mention later; for now we'll present it in rough form.

この部屋を片付けるには時間がかかるので一応机の上だけでもき
れいにしておこう。

It's going to take time to straighten up this room, so I'll just clean off the
top of the desk for the time being.

ie 言え See **to wa ie**

ieba 言えば See **to ieba**

ieba ... da 言えば〜だ See **to ieba ... (da)**

ieba ieru 言えば言える See **to ieba ieru**

iedomo 言えども See **to iedomo**

ii ga ... nara いいが〜なら See **mo ii ga ... nara**

ijō (wa)　以上（は）

> as long as; so long as
> Similar to: *kara (ni) wa*
>
> X *ijō (wa)* Y
> As long as X is the case, then Y follows.
>
> See also: **kagiri (1)**; **ue wa**

この会社の社員である<u>以上（は）</u>、会社の規則に従わないわけには

いかない。

As long as I am an employee of this company, I cannot very well fail to
follow the company rules.

アメリカで生活する<u>以上（は）</u>英語が出来なければならないという
考えは、今日では必ずしも通用しない。

The idea that as long as one lives in the United States one must speak
English does not necessarily hold today.

ika ni　如何に

(1)
> how; in what way
> Similar to: *dono yō ni*

いじめをする子供を<u>如何に</u>扱うべきか、困っている。

We are troubled by how we should handle children who bully.

この調査の結果を<u>如何に</u>解釈するかは個人によって違うであろう。

How one interprets the results of this investigation will differ according
to the person.

(2) | how much; to what degree
Similar to: *donna ni*; *dore dake*

この本が<u>如何に</u>おもしろいかは<ruby>読<rt>よ</rt></ruby>んでみないとわからない。

You won't know how interesting this book is unless you read it.

これは<u>如何に</u>頭がよくても、勉強しないで百点がとれるような試験ではない。

No matter how smart you may be, this is not the kind of test where you can get a hundred without studying.

ikkan shite　一貫して

consistently; constantly

X *wa ikkan shite* Y
X is consistently Y. Suggests that things remain the same from X to Y.
A semi-idiomatic use of the gerund of *ikkan-suru*, meaning "be consistent."

<ruby>山田教授<rt>やまだきょうじゅ</rt></ruby>の<ruby>講義<rt>こうぎ</rt></ruby>は<u>一貫して</u><ruby>退屈<rt>たいくつ</rt></ruby>であると言ってもよい。

It is fair to say that Professor Yamada's lectures are consistently boring.

<ruby>彼女<rt>かのじょ</rt></ruby>の日本<ruby>文学研究<rt>ぶんがくけんきゅう</rt></ruby>におけるテーマは<u>一貫して</u><ruby>源氏物語<rt>げんじものがたり</rt></ruby>をもとにしたものであった。

The themes in her research on Japanese literature were consistently based on *The Tale of Genji*.

36

imasara . . . -nai いまさら〜-ない［今更〜-ない］

> too late to; at this belated time; now
> Similar to: *ima ni natte . . . -nai; mohaya . . . -nai*

もう済んだことだから、今更グチをこぼしても仕方がない。

It's over, so it's useless to complain at this point.

あの時もう少しがんばっていれば合格したのであろうが、今更
後悔してもはじまらない。

If I had worked a little harder at that time, I would have passed, but it's
too late for regrets now.

imi de 意味で

> in the sense of
>
> X (to iu) imi de Y
> In the sense of X, Y is the case. The statement in Y is to be
> comprehended by what is said in X. It can also be used to mean
> "for the purpose of," as in the second example below.

出島は鎖国時代西洋と日本のあいだのかけ橋であった（という）
意味で重要な存在であった。

Dejima played an important role in the sense that it was a link between
the West and Japan during the period of national seclusion.

試験は、学生に勉強させる（という）意味で、なくてはならないも
のである。

For the purpose of getting students to study, exams are necessary.

imi suru　意味する

> X *wa* Y *o imi suru*
> X means Y.
>
> See also: **koto ni naru (2)**; **wake da**

<ruby>円高<rt>えんだか</rt></ruby>ドル<ruby>安<rt>やす</rt></ruby>であるということは、日本から<ruby>多<rt>おお</rt></ruby>くの<ruby>旅行者<rt>りょこうしゃ</rt></ruby>がやって
くるということを<u>意味する</u>。

The fact that the yen is high against the dollar means that large numbers of Japanese tourists will come.

<ruby>今年<rt>ことし</rt></ruby>の<ruby>冬<rt>ふゆ</rt></ruby>は<ruby>雪<rt>ゆき</rt></ruby>も<ruby>少<rt>すく</rt></ruby>なく<ruby>雨<rt>あめ</rt></ruby>もほとんど<ruby>降<rt>ふ</rt></ruby>らなかった。これは<ruby>夏<rt>なつ</rt></ruby>、<ruby>水<rt>みず</rt></ruby>
<ruby>不足<rt>ぶそく</rt></ruby>になるということを<u>意味する</u>。

This winter there was little snow and it hardly rained.　This means that there will be a shortage of water this summer.

ina ya　否や　See **ya ina ya**

irai　以来

> since; following (with regard to temporal matters)
>
> X *irai*
> Where X is a verb, V-*te irai* is similar to V-*te kara* and means "after, since V."
> Where X is a noun, N *irai* is similar to N *kara* and means "since, after N." Where X is a period of time, X *irai* does not mean from the end of the period.　Thus, Meiji (1868-1912) *irai* does not mean after 1912, but from 1868 or some point during the period.

<ruby>彼<rt>かれ</rt></ruby>は日本から<ruby>帰<rt>かえ</rt></ruby>って<u>以来</u>、<ruby>真面目<rt>まじめ</rt></ruby>に日本<ruby>美術<rt>びじゅつ</rt></ruby>の<ruby>研究<rt>けんきゅう</rt></ruby>に<ruby>取<rt>と</rt></ruby>り<ruby>組<rt>く</rt></ruby>むようになった。

Since he got back from Japan, he has become seriously involved in the study of Japanese art.

<ruby>阪神大震災<rt>はんしんだいしんさい</rt></ruby><u>以来</u>、日本では<ruby>地震対策<rt>じしんたいさく</rt></ruby>が<ruby>問題<rt>もんだい</rt></ruby>になっている。

Since the Great Kobe Earthquake, earthquake policy in Japan has become an issue.

<ruby>彼女<rt>かのじょ</rt></ruby>は<ruby>去年<rt>きょねん</rt></ruby>の<ruby>三月<rt>さんがつ</rt></ruby><u>以来</u>、私に<ruby>怒<rt>おこ</rt></ruby>っているらしく、<ruby>口<rt>くち</rt></ruby>すらきいてくれない。

Since March of last year, she has appeared to be angry with me and won't even speak to me.

issai . . . -nai　一切〜-ない

> absolutely not; none whatsoever
> Similar to: *mattaku . . . -nai*; *zenzen . . . -nai*
>
> *issai* V-*nai*
> Absolute negation of V. When the verb is *aru*, the negative is *nai* alone, as in the first example below.

あの<ruby>教授<rt>きょうじゅ</rt></ruby>の<ruby>授業<rt>じゅぎょう</rt></ruby>は<ruby>非常<rt>ひじょう</rt></ruby>におもしろいので、<ruby>授業中<rt>じゅぎょうちゅう</rt></ruby>に<ruby>居眠<rt>いねむ</rt></ruby>りする学生など<u>一切ない</u>。

That professor's classes are very interesting, so not a single student falls asleep during them.

パーティーの席<ruby>席<rt>せき</rt></ruby>で飲み過<ruby>過<rt>す</rt></ruby>ぎたため、どうやって家<ruby>家<rt>いえ</rt></ruby>に帰<ruby>帰<rt>かえ</rt></ruby>りついたのか、一切覚<ruby>覚<rt>おぼ</rt></ruby>えて<u>ない</u>。

I drank too much at the party, and I've no idea at all how I got home.

itaru to　至ると　See **ni itaru to**

itatte wa　至っては　See **ni itaru to**

itsu no ma ni ka　いつの間にか

> without being aware of something; before one knows it; in no time
> Similar to: *itsu ka shiranai uchi ni*

明日締切<ruby>締切<rt>しめき</rt></ruby>りのレポートを書いているうちに、<u>いつの間にか</u>夜<ruby>夜<rt>よ</rt></ruby>が明<ruby>明<rt>あ</rt></ruby>けてきた。

When I was writing a paper that was due the next day, it became dawn before I knew it.

子供<ruby>子供<rt>こども</rt></ruby>を日本に連れて行<ruby>行<rt>つ</rt></ruby>ったところ、<u>いつの間にか</u>日本語を上手<ruby>上手<rt>じょうず</rt></ruby>に話すようになった。

When I took my child to Japan, in no time at all s/he had become proficient in Japanese.

40

ittai . . . ka   一体〜か

> What/Who/How (etc.) in the world!
>
> Often used with question words to convey exasperation about something that is truly incomprehensible. Commonly *zentai* is added following *ittai*.

そのような学生の態度を我々は<u>一体</u>どう解釈すべきであろう<u>か</u>。

How in the world are we to understand the attitude of that kind of student?

賃上げ要求のストライキをすると言うのは<u>一体</u>全体誰が言い出したことなの<u>か</u>誰も分からなかった。

Nobody knew who in the world it was who first came up with the idea of striking for salary increases.

ittara nai   言ったらない   See **to ittara nai**

itta yō na mono   いったようなもの   See **to itta yō na mono**

itte (mo) ii   言って（も）いい   See **to itte (mo) ii**

itte (mo) ii kurai   言って（も）いいくらい   See **to itte (mo) ii kurai**

itte (mo) yoi   言って（も）よい   See **to itte (mo) ii**

41

iu ka いうか See **to iu ka**

iu koto いうこと See **to iu koto**

iu made mo nai 言うまでもない

> needless to say; it goes without saying
>
> X *wa iu made mo nai*
> X is regarded as a matter of course and there is no need even to mention it.
>
> See also: **made (4)**

<ruby>多<rt>おお</rt></ruby>くの<ruby>人々<rt>ひとびと</rt></ruby>が<ruby>先日<rt>せんじつ</rt></ruby>の<ruby>株価<rt>かぶか</rt></ruby>の<ruby>急落<rt>きゅうらく</rt></ruby>によって非常な<ruby>打撃<rt>だげき</rt></ruby>を<ruby>受<rt>う</rt></ruby>けたことは言うまでもない。

The sudden fall in stock values the other day gave quite a few people a severe jolt, needless to say.

<ruby>仕事<rt>しごと</rt></ruby>を<ruby>探<rt>さが</rt></ruby>す<ruby>場合<rt>ばあい</rt></ruby>、<ruby>学歴<rt>がくれき</rt></ruby>がものをいうことは言うまでもない。

Needless to say, one's academic history is a key factor in looking for a job.

iu no wa いうのは See **to iu no wa**

iwanu made mo 言わぬまでも See **to (wa) iwanu made mo**

iwan ya . . . ni oite o ya　いわんや～においてをや

> all the more; even more so
> Similar to: *mochiron*
>
> X. *Iwan ya* Y *ni oite o ya*, where X and Y are contrasting nouns.
> Whatever holds for X holds even more for Y. There is an element
> of escalation in this pattern.
>
> See also: **mashite**

<ruby>近頃<rt>ちかごろ</rt></ruby>、<ruby>不景気<rt>ふけいき</rt></ruby>で<ruby>大企業<rt>だいぎょう</rt></ruby>も<ruby>苦<rt>くる</rt></ruby>しんでいる。いわんや<ruby>小企業<rt>しょうきぎょう</rt></ruby>においてをや。

Now when even big business is suffering from recession, smaller
companies are suffering even more.

<ruby>中堅層<rt>ちゅうけんそう</rt></ruby>の<ruby>指導者<rt>しどうしゃ</rt></ruby>も<ruby>政治<rt>せいじ</rt></ruby>に<ruby>関心<rt>かんしん</rt></ruby>を<ruby>示<rt>しめ</rt></ruby>さなくなった。いわんや<ruby>若者<rt>わかもの</rt></ruby>においてをや。

Even middle-aged leaders no longer show an interest in politics. So what
do you expect of young people!

iwarete iru　言われている　See to iwarete iru

iwazu . . . iwazu　言わず～言わず　See to iwazu . . . to iwazu

i wa shinai　いはしない　See wa shinai

izen to shite　依然として

> still; as before
>
> X *wa izen to shite* Y
> X still remains Y. Indicates an unchanged situation.

<ruby>彼女<rt>かのじょ</rt></ruby>が<ruby>家出<rt>いえで</rt></ruby>をしてから、もう<ruby>一週間<rt>いっしゅうかん</rt></ruby>になるが、彼女の<ruby>行方<rt>ゆくえ</rt></ruby>は<u>依然
として</u>わからない。

It has been a week since she left home, but her whereabouts still remain
unknown.

バミューダトライアングルは<u>依然として</u><ruby>謎<rt>なぞ</rt></ruby>である。

The Bermuda Triangle remains as much a mystery as before.

J

-jō　-上

> (1) from the perspective of . . . ; in view of . . .
>
> N-*jō*
> From the perspective of N. -*Jō* can be used either adverbially or as
> a noun modifier with *no* following it.
>
> See also: **ue de (1)**

<ruby>明治<rt>めいじ</rt></ruby>は日本の<ruby>近代化<rt>きんだいか</rt></ruby>において<ruby>歴史<rt>れきし</rt></ruby><u>上</u>、<ruby>重要<rt>じゅうよう</rt></ruby>な<ruby>時代<rt>じだい</rt></ruby>であった。

From the perspective of history, Meiji was an important period in the
modernization of Japan.

44

<ruby>今回<rt>こんかい</rt></ruby>の<ruby>選挙<rt>せんきよ</rt></ruby>で<ruby>保守<rt>ほしゅ</rt></ruby><ruby>派<rt>は</rt></ruby>が<ruby>勝利<rt>しょうり</rt></ruby>をおさめたのは、<ruby>国内情勢<rt>こくないじょうせい</rt></ruby><u>上</u>、<ruby>当然<rt>とうぜん</rt></ruby>の

ことであったといえるであろう。

It can no doubt be said that the conservatives' win in the recent elections was the natural outcome, in view of domestic conditions.

---

(2)   due to; because of

N-*jō*
Because of X.
Jō can be used either adverbially or as a noun-modifier with *no* following it.

<ruby>兄<rt>あに</rt></ruby>が大学を<ruby>辞<rt>や</rt></ruby>めたのは<ruby>経済<rt>けいざい</rt></ruby><u>上</u>の<ruby>理由<rt>りゆう</rt></ruby>ではなく、<ruby>学問<rt>がくもん</rt></ruby><u>上</u>の理由から

であった。

My brother's quitting college was not due to financial but to academic reasons.

日本では、山が<ruby>多<rt>おお</rt></ruby>く<ruby>国土<rt>こくど</rt></ruby>が<ruby>狭<rt>せま</rt></ruby>い<ruby>関係<rt>かんけい</rt></ruby><u>上</u>、<ruby>河川<rt>かせん</rt></ruby>は<ruby>皆<rt>みな</rt></ruby><ruby>短<rt>みじか</rt></ruby>くて<ruby>流<rt>なが</rt></ruby>れが<ruby>速<rt>はや</rt></ruby>い。

Because of the many mountains and small land area of Japan, the rivers are all short and their currents are swift.

K

-ka -家

---

(1)   N-*ka*
A specialist in N.
This *ka* is a suffix that attaches to a noun that represents a field of work and indicates one who specializes in that field.

私は息子が政治家になるよりも、芸術家になって欲しいと常に望んでいる。

I have always wished that my son would become an artist rather than a politician.

---

(2) | N-*ka*
A suffix suggesting that a person is characterized by N, where N is a descriptive noun.

彼は稀にみる情熱家である。

He is the kind of passionate person you rarely see.

田中さんは楽天家と言われるだけあって、自分の勤めている会社が倒産寸前であるというのに、ゆうゆうとしている。

Tanaka deserves her/his reputation as an optimist, because s/he is not upset even though the company where s/he works is on the verge of bankruptcy.

kaette　かえって

| on the contrary; rather
Similar to: *gyaku ni*

Suggests something contrary to what one might have thought.

彼女は褒めてもらえると思って、正直にありのままを話したところ、かえって、怒られてしまった。

She spoke honestly of the way things were, thinking she would be praised, but on the contrary she was scolded.

<ruby>子<rt>こ</rt></ruby><ruby>供<rt>ども</rt></ruby>を<ruby>無<rt>む</rt></ruby><ruby>理<rt>り</rt></ruby>に勉強させるのは、<u>かえって</u>、よくない。

Contrary to what one might think, forcing children to study is not good.

kagiranai 限らない See **to (wa) kagiranai**

kagirazu 限らず See **ni kagirazu**

kagiri 限り

(1)
> as long as; so long as
> Similar to: *aida wa; uchi wa*
>
> X *kagiri* Y
> Y as long as X. When X is in the negative, the expression means "so long as X is not the case." This is often best rendered as "unless X is the case," as in the second example below.
>
> See also: **ijō (wa); ue wa**

<ruby>民<rt>みん</rt></ruby><ruby>主<rt>しゅ</rt></ruby><ruby>政<rt>せい</rt></ruby><ruby>府<rt>ふ</rt></ruby>が<ruby>続<rt>つづ</rt></ruby>く<u>限り</u>、日本は<ruby>安<rt>あん</rt></ruby><ruby>泰<rt>たい</rt></ruby>である。

Japan will be peaceful as long as democratic rule continues.

<ruby>田<rt>た</rt></ruby><ruby>中<rt>なか</rt></ruby>さんは<ruby>酒<rt>さけ</rt></ruby>とたばこをやめない<u>限り</u>、元気になるまい。

Tanaka is not likely to feel well unless s/he stops drinking and smoking.

(2)
> as much as possible
>
> V *kagiri*, where V is in the potential form.
> As much V as possible; as much as one can V. Sets the limit for V. Often used as a noun modifier with *no* following it.

47

しばらく旅行^{りょこう}に出^でかけるので、持^もてる<u>限り</u>のものをスーツケースにつめこんだ。

I'll be traveling for some time, so I crammed as many things as I could possibly carry into my suitcase.

息子^{むすこ}の教育^{きょういく}に関^{かん}しては、出来^{でき}る<u>限り</u>のことをしたいと思っている。

With regard to my son's education, I want to do as much as I possibly can.

kagitte 限って See **ni kagiri**

-kakaru -かかる

---

in the midst of; halfway; be about to

V-stem-*kakaru*
In the midst of V; halfway V; be about to V.
As in the first example, when used as a noun modifier this pattern is similar to -*kake no*.

See also: **-kake no**

こんなに壊^{こわ}れ<u>かかった</u>車^{くるま}で遠^{とお}くまで行くのは無理^{むり}であろう。

I don't think it's possible to go a long distance in such a rundown car.

彼女^{かのじょ}に頼^{たの}まれたケーキが今出来^{いまでき}<u>かかって</u>いる。

The cake she requested is almost done.

kakawarazu かかわらず See **ni (mo) kakawarazu**

48

-kake no -かけの

---

half-done; incomplete; unfinished

V-stem-*kake no* N
An N that is half V-ed.
Expresses something that is not yet completed.

See also: **-kakaru**

食べかけの魚を猫にやった。

I gave the half-eaten fish to the cat.

その作家の死後、ノートの中から書きかけの詩が発見された。

After that writer's death, unfinished poems were discovered among his/her notes.

-kakeru -かける[-掛ける]

---

begin to; in the process of; be about to; be on the point of
Similar to V-stem-*hajimeru*; V-*sō ni naru*

V-stem-*kakeru*
Expresses the beginning of an action, something in process, or something that is about to occur.

See also: **-dasu (1)**

彼は言いかけて辞めた。

He started to speak, then stopped.

49

ちょうど宿題^{しゅくだい}をやり<u>かけていた</u>ところへ友達^{ともだち}がきてできなくなった。

Just when I began doing my homework, a friend came over, and I was unable to keep working at it.

私は三年ぐらい前に死^しに<u>かけた</u>ことがある。

I almost died about three years ago.

kakete かけて See **ni kakete**

kakete wa かけては See **ni kakete wa**

kanarazu shimo . . . -nai 必ずしも〜-ない

> not necessarily
> Similar to: *kanarazu . . . to iu wake de wa nai*
>
> *kanarazu shimo X-nai*
> Not necessarily X.

ブランド品^{ひん}が<u>必ずしも</u>いいとは限^{かぎ}<u>らない</u>。

Brand-name products are not necessarily good.

アメリカにおける東^{ひがし}アジア言語文化研究^{げん ご ぶん か けんきゅう}において、私立大学^{し りつ}が州^{しゅう}立大学^{りつ}よりいいとは<u>必ずしも</u>言え<u>ない</u>。

It isn't necessarily true that private universities are better than state universities in research on East Asian languages and cultures in the United States.

50

-kanenai   -かねない［-兼ねない］

> is likely to; may be the case
>
> V-stem-*kanenai*
> Is likely to V; V may be the case; cannot say V won't happen.
> Often used in describing unfavorable situations.

こんなに雨が少なくては水不足になり<u>かねない</u>。

Since we have had so little rain, it is likely that there will be a water shortage.

あの人は気が弱いので友達に頼まれると断り切れないで悪いことでも<u>しかねない</u>。

That person is so timid that s/he cannot say no and is even apt to do something bad if asked by a friend.

-kaneru   -かねる［-兼ねる］

> cannot; be unable to; be in no position to; hesitate to
>
> V-stem-*kaneru*
> Indicates that V cannot be done, even if one wanted to.

この件に関しては山本さんが一番よく知っているはずだが、あまりよく彼女を知らないので電話<u>しかね</u>ている。

I expect that on this subject Yamamoto is the most knowledgeable, but I don't know her very well and so I'm hesitating to call her.

51

田中さんが大学入試に落ちたことを知ったばかりだ。彼の気持を
考えると自分が合格したことをどうも<u>言いかねて</u>しまう。

I just found out that Tanaka failed his university entrance exam. When I
consider his feelings, I simply can't bear to tell him that I passed.

kanshite   関して   See ni kanshite

kansuru   関する   See ni kansuru

kara koso   からこそ

---

especially because; in particular because

X *kara koso* Y
With emphatic *koso* added to *kara* the meaning becomes "precisely
because of X, then Y."
X is emphasized as the one and only cause of Y.

See also: **koso**

コーチの言う通りにした<u>からこそ</u>、夕べの試合に勝つことができ
たのだ。

We won the game last night because we did exactly what our coach told us.

この辺は夜、危険だ<u>からこそ</u>、もう少し街灯を多くするべきだ。

Precisely because this area is dangerous at night, we should have more
street lights.

52

-karō **-かろう**

> probably
> Similar to: *darō*
>
> X-*karō*, where X is an adjective stem (including the negative form -*nai*).
> X may be the case; probably X.
>
> See also: **de arō**

この<ruby>辺<rt>へん</rt></ruby>にはそんな<ruby>高級<rt>こうきゅう</rt></ruby>な<ruby>店<rt>みせ</rt></ruby>などなか<u>ろう</u>。

That kind of high-class store or anything like it probably wouldn't be located around here.

<ruby>講演<rt>こうえん</rt></ruby>は<ruby>十時<rt>じゅうじ</rt></ruby>に<ruby>始<rt>はじ</rt></ruby>まるということだが、<ruby>少<rt>すこ</rt></ruby>しぐらい<ruby>遅<rt>おく</rt></ruby>れて行っても

よ<u>かろう</u>。

I understand that the lecture is going to begin at ten o'clock, but I think it is probably all right to get there a little late.

<ruby>新<rt>あたら</rt></ruby>しいフランスの<ruby>映画<rt>えいが</rt></ruby>はおもしろ<u>かろう</u>と思って行ってみたが、

それほどでもなかった。

I thought the new French movie would probably be interesting and went to see it, but it wasn't as interesting as I thought it would be.

ka to **かと**

> X *ka to* Y
> Y usually expresses concern over whether X might come about. X is often in the negative.

友達にいやなことを言われるのではない<u>かと</u>気になる。

I am worried for fear that I might be told something unpleasant by my friend.

弟は、そのニュースを聞いたとたんに泣き出すのではない<u>か</u>と思う。

I'm wondering whether my younger brother will burst into tears the moment he hears the news.

ka to mireba   かとみれば   See   ka to miru to

ka to miru to   かとみると

> as soon as; no sooner . . . than
>
> V-*ta ka to miru to* X
> Just when V, X; simultaneously with V, X occurs. V and X occur almost, but not quite, simultaneously.
>
> See also: **ga hayai ka; nari (1); totan (ni); ya ina ya**

突然大風が吹き出した<u>かとみると</u>、あっという間に屋根がふきとばされてしまった。

No sooner did a strong wind suddenly begin to blow than the roof was blown off.

いなびかりがした<u>かとみると</u>、うちの前の大木が真二つに割かれてしまった。

There was a flash of lightning, and just then the big tree in front of our house split in two.

54

kawari ni 代わりに

> in place of; instead of; in exchange for; in compensation for
>
> X *no kawari ni* Y, where *no* is used when X is a noun.
> In place of X, Y; in exchange for X, Y. X may be implied, as in the
> second example below.

怪我をした友人の代わりに、テニスの試合に出ることになった。

It was arranged that I would play in the tennis match in place of my
friend, who was injured.

日本に留学していた時、日本人の友達が日本語を教えてくれたの
で、代わりに私は英語を教えた。

While I was studying in Japan, my Japanese friend taught me Japanese,
so in exchange I taught him/her English.

このカメラは安い代わりにすぐこわれそうだ。

This camera is cheap, but as part of the bargain it looks like it will break
right away.

宿題にスタインベックの『怒りの葡萄』を読むことになっている
が、本を読む代わりにビデオを借りて見ようと思っている。

I'm supposed to read Steinbeck's *The Grapes of Wrath* for homework,
but instead of reading the book, I'm thinking of renting the video and
watching it.

ki 気 See **Appendix A** for a list of idioms and example sentences using *ki*

kimatte iru　決まっている　See **ni kimatte iru**

ki ni naru　気になる

(1)	weigh on the mind; be worrisome X *ga ki ni naru* X weighs on the mind or is a source of concern.

きのう喧嘩した友達に電話をしようと思うが、まだ怒っているの
ではないかと気になる。

I thought I would call the friend I had an argument with yesterday, but
I'm afraid that s/he might still be angry.

今日の面接のことが気になって、夕べぜんぜん眠れなかった。

Worried about today's interview, I was unable to sleep at all last night.

(2)	feel like V *ki ni naru*, where V is in the citation form. Feel like V-ing.

早朝のジョギングは健康にいいというが、どうしても早起きする
気にならない。

They say that early morning jogging is good for the health, but I just
don't feel like getting up early.

56

日本に行っている友達の話を聞いて、私も日本語を勉強する<u>気に</u>
<u>なった</u>。

Hearing the stories of my friend who had gone to Japan, I got the urge to
study Japanese.

ki ni suru　気にする

> worry; be concerned about
>
> X *ga* Y *o ki ni suru*
> X worries about Y.
> Unlike *ki ni naru* (above), which describes a psychological state,
> with *ki ni suru*, volition is indicated. One is conscious of a matter
> with *ki ni suru*, whereas *ki ni naru* suggests less conscious
> involvement.

人のことばかり<u>気にしている</u>と、何も出来ない。

If you just worry about others, you won't be able to do anything.

子供が十時ごろまでに帰ってくるなら、あまり<u>気にする</u>必要はない
が、それより遅く帰ってくるようだったら、少し<u>気にした</u>方がいい。

It's not necessary to worry as long as your children come home by about
ten, but if it appears that it will be later than that, you had better worry.

-kiru　-切る

> finish; (be) completely
> Similar to: *owaru*
>
> V-stem-*kiru*
> Finish V; V completely

疲れ<u>切って</u>もう一歩も歩けない。

I am completely exhausted and can't walk another step.

こんなに厚い本はとても一晩では<u>読み切れない</u>。

I can't possibly finish reading such a thick book in one night.

kitara きたら See to kitara

konasu こなす

> skillfully; with ease
> Similar to: *jōzu ni dekiru*
>
> V-stem *konasu*
> Able to V with skill; able to V with ease; able to V easily.
> Also used without a preceding verb, as in the third example below.
> Potential form is *konaseru*, with the same meaning.

ジョーンズさんは日本語を始めてまだ二年しか経っていないが、古文でも上手に読み<u>こなす</u>。

It has only been two years since Jones began Japanese, but s/he can even read the classical language well.

モーツァルトのオペラが歌い<u>こなせる</u>ようになるまでには、大変な努力が必要である。

It is necessary to make great efforts to get to the point where you can sing Mozart operas skillfully.

佐藤さんはスポーツなら何でも<u>こなして</u>しまう。

When it comes to sports, Satō can do everything.

koso こそ

---

precisely; indeed

X *koso*
Emphatic expression strengthening X.

See also: **kara koso**

<ruby>京都<rt></rt></ruby>こそ日本の<ruby>伝統的<rt>でんとうてき</rt></ruby>な<ruby>町<rt>まち</rt></ruby>である。

Kyoto is *the* traditional city of Japan.

<ruby>忍耐<rt>にんたい</rt></ruby>こそ日本人の<ruby>美徳<rt>びとく</rt></ruby>と<ruby>考<rt>かんが</rt></ruby>える人も<ruby>多<rt>おお</rt></ruby>い。

Many people consider patience to be *the* Japanese virtue.

koto こと

Used in many ways in Japanese sentences, but here we emphasize its use as an imperative at the end of sentences.

<ruby>九時半<rt>くじはん</rt></ruby>の<ruby>電車<rt>でんしゃ</rt></ruby>に<ruby>乗<rt>の</rt></ruby>るので、九時までに<ruby>駅<rt>えき</rt></ruby>の前に<ruby>集合<rt>しゅうごう</rt></ruby>する<u>こと</u>。

Since we are taking the 9:30 train, be sure to meet us in front of the station by 9:00.

<ruby>明日<rt></rt></ruby>は<ruby>血液検査<rt>けつえきけんさ</rt></ruby>をするので、<ruby>今晩<rt>こんばん</rt></ruby>は<ruby>何<rt>なに</rt></ruby>も<ruby>食<rt>た</rt></ruby>べない<u>こと</u>。

Because you are going to have a blood test tomorrow, make sure that you don't eat anything tonight.

koto (de) こと（で） See **no koto (de)**

koto ga aru ことがある

> The pattern V-*ta koto ga aru* is a well-known way to express "(I)
> have had the experience of . . . " With the verb in the citation form,
> however, the meaning is "There are times when . . . "
>
> See also: **koto wa nai**

生まれ育った町を離れてもう二十年になるが、まだその町に住ん
でいる幼友達のことを思い出す<u>ことがある</u>。

It has been twenty years since I left the town where I was raised, but there
are times when I think of my childhood friends who are still living there.

外食はあまりしないことにしているが、和食は食べに行く<u>ことが
ある</u>。

I make it a rule not to eat out very often, but there are times when I do go
out to eat Japanese food.

koto ka ことか

> An exclamatory ending used with interrogative words that mean
> "how much," such as *donna ni* and *ika ni*.

日本の正月はどんなに賑やかな<u>ことか</u>。

How lively the Japanese New Year is!

兄は酒を飲まないようになってから、どんなに元気になった<u>ことか</u>。

How healthy my older brother has become since he stopped drinking!

koto ni naru　　こ と に な る

---

(1) | X *koto ni naru*
Indicates changes, decisions, or developments apart from an
individual's will.

この<ruby>三月<rt>さんがつ</rt></ruby>で私はこの<ruby>町<rt>まち</rt></ruby>に<ruby>五年す<rt>ごねんす</rt></ruby>んでいる<u>ことになる</u>。

This March it will be (it comes to) five years that I have lived in this town.

<ruby>来年<rt>らいねん</rt></ruby>の<ruby>五月<rt>ごがつ</rt></ruby>から<ruby>三年間<rt>さんねんかん</rt></ruby>、フランスに<ruby>単身赴任<rt>たんしんふにん</rt></ruby>する<u>ことになった</u>。

It was decided that I will go to France to work for three years beginning

in May of next year, leaving my family behind.

---

(2) | X *(to iu) koto ni naru*
X means; X amounts to or means such and such, where a
conclusion is drawn from an existing situation.

See also: **imi suru**; **wake da**

AはBより大きく、BはCより大きいなら、AはCより大きい

（という）<u>ことになる</u>。

If A is bigger than B and B is bigger than C, then A is bigger than C.

koto ni naru to　　こ と に な る と　See **to iu koto ni naru to**; **to naru to**

koto ni natte iru　ことになっている

> it is the practice; it is the custom; it is the way it is
>
> X *koto ni natte iru*
> X has been decided upon and it has become a regular practice.
> Unlike with *koto ni shite iru*, it is not something that one actively
> does oneself. X has become a custom or fixed practice apart from
> an individual's will.
>
> See also: **mono to kimatte iru**

日本では、レストランでもチップを払わないことになっている。

In Japan it is the custom not to leave tips, even at restaurants.

日本では、二十になったら、酒を飲んでもいいことになっている。

In Japan, the acceptable age for beginning to drink alcohol is twenty.

koto ni shita　ことにした　See **yō ni suru**

koto ni shite iru　ことにしている

> make it a rule; make it a practice; make it a habit to do such and
> such
>
> V *koto ni shite iru*, where V is either positive or negative.
> It is one's habit to do V. In contrast, in V *yō ni shite iru*, one is
> making efforts to do V, but it has not become a habit or a routine.

一日もはやく元気になるように、毎日散歩をすることにしている。

I make it a practice to take a walk every day, in order to get healthy as

soon as possible.

眠_{ねむ}れなくなると困_{こま}るので、夜_{よる}コーヒーを飲まない<u>ことにしている</u>。

I make it a rule not to drink coffee at night, because I hate it when I can't fall asleep.

koto ni suru　ことにする　See *yō ni suru*

koto ni (wa)　ことに(は)

X *koto ni (wa)* Y
Y is the reason that causes the state or emotion expressed by X. Used in expressing emotions emphatically and follows both positive and negative statements.

ありがたい<u>ことに(は)</u>、うちの子_こは、礼儀_{れいぎ}をわきまえている。

Fortunately [or I am grateful that], my child is well behaved.

西田_{にしだ}さんに電話_{でんわ}をしなければならないが、こまった<u>ことに(は)</u>、電話番号_{ばんごう}がわからない。

I must call Nishida but unfortunately I don't know his/her number.

驚_{おどろ}いた<u>ことに(は)</u>、アメリカ人のスミスさんの方_{ほう}が普通_{ふつう}の日本人よりずっと漢字を知_しっている。

To my surprise, Smith, an American, knows many more *kanji* than the average Japanese.

koto wa　ことは

> X *koto wa* X
> It is accepted that X is the case, but a negative qualification
> follows.
>
> See also:　**aru ni wa aru**

うちの子は体は大きい<u>ことは</u>大きいが、まだまだ子供でこまる。

It is certainly true that my child is big, but I am afraid that s/he is still
immature.

スミスさんは、日本語の授業に出ている<u>ことは</u>出ているが、全然
予習復習していないようだ。

Smith is going to his/her Japanese class all right, but it seems that s/he
doesn't prepare or review at all.

koto wa nai　ことはない

> V *koto wa nai*
> Very strong, complete negation of V. Where V is in the past (*-ta*
> form), the sense is "have never V-ed."
>
> See also:　**koto ga aru**

日本では刑法上の罪を犯さない限り、仕事をやめさせられる<u>こと
はない</u>と言われている。

It is said that in Japan you'll never get fired as long as you don't commit a
criminal offense.

君は何も悪いことをしていないのだから、誰にもとやかく言われ<ruby>きみ<rt></rt></ruby><ruby>わる<rt></rt></ruby><ruby>だれ<rt></rt></ruby>
<u>ることはない</u>。

You have done nothing wrong, so there is nothing for which you can be criticized by anyone.

kurabete 比べて See **ni kurabete**

kurai くらい

> to the extent of; limited to; just about.
>
> Although often used to express approximation with numbers as in "about ten people" *(jūnin kurai)*, the term is also used to express extent or degree and is similar in meaning to *hodo*. It occurs in both positive and negative sentences, and is often used in comparisons.
>
> See also: **hodo; to itte (mo) ii kurai**

日本語の出来るアメリカ人をたくさん知っているが、辞書をひか
ないで日本語の新聞が読めるのはジョーンズさん<u>くらい</u>のものだ。

I know many Americans who know Japanese, but Jones is just about the only one who can read Japanese newspapers without using a dictionary.

言語の中でペルシャ語<u>くらい</u>難しいものはないと言われる。

It is said that among languages none is as difficult as Persian.

kuru to くると See **to kuru to**

kuse shite　くせして

---

in spite of; although
Similar to: *kuse ni*

X *(no) kuse shite* Y, where *no* is used when X is a noun.
Y expresses something that one would expect of X but is not the case.

See also: **ni mo kakawarazu; no ni (1)**

<ruby>山本<rt>やまもと</rt></ruby>さんは日本人の<u>くせして</u>、おすしも<ruby>刺身<rt>さしみ</rt></ruby>も食べない。

Even though Yamamoto is Japanese, s/he doesn't eat either sushi or sashimi.

<ruby>鈴木<rt>すずき</rt></ruby>さんはオランダに<ruby>長<rt>なが</rt></ruby>いこと<ruby>住<rt>す</rt></ruby>んでいた<u>くせして</u>、オランダ<ruby>語<rt>ご</rt></ruby>が<ruby>全然出来<rt>ぜんぜんでき</rt></ruby>ない。

Although Suzuki lived in Holland for a long time, s/he doesn't know Dutch at all.

M

made　まで

In addition to the usages of *made* to indicate "up to" with reference to both time and location, there are the following usages:

(1) extent; as far as; so far as

V-*te made* X, where X is negative.
V expresses an extreme case, and *made* indicates that one need not go that far.

<ruby>体<rt>からだ</rt></ruby>をこわしてまでダイエットすべきではない。

You shouldn't diet to the point of destroying your health.

<ruby>嘘<rt>うそ</rt></ruby>をついてまで<ruby>我<rt>わ</rt></ruby>が<ruby>子<rt>こ</rt></ruby>の<ruby>肩<rt>かた</rt></ruby>を持つ<ruby>必要<rt>ひつよう</rt></ruby>はない。

It's not necessary to take the side of one's child to the point of lying (on his/her behalf).

(2) even
Similar to: *mo*

X *made* Y
X is something one would not expect to be related to Y but is used with *made* to emphasize to what lengths Y is the case.

やさしい<ruby>数学<rt>すうがく</rt></ruby>の<ruby>問題<rt>もんだい</rt></ruby>が<ruby>解<rt>と</rt></ruby>けないで、<ruby>小<rt>ちい</rt></ruby>さい<ruby>子供<rt>こども</rt></ruby>にまで<ruby>馬鹿<rt>ばか</rt></ruby>にされた。

Unable to solve easy math problems, I was made fun of even by small children.

<ruby>親友<rt>しんゆう</rt></ruby>の<ruby>山本<rt>やまもと</rt></ruby>さんまで私が<ruby>盗<rt>ぬす</rt></ruby>みをはたらいたと思っている。

Even my close friend Yamamoto thinks I committed theft.

(3) only; merely
Similar to: *tada sore dake*

N *made (ni)*
No more than N; just N.

ご<ruby>注意<rt>ちゅうい</rt></ruby>まで(に)<ruby>申<rt>もう</rt></ruby>し<ruby>上<rt>あ</rt></ruby>げておくが、この<ruby>辺<rt>へん</rt></ruby>は<ruby>夜危<rt>よるあぶ</rt></ruby>ないので<ruby>気<rt>き</rt></ruby>を<ruby>付<rt>つ</rt></ruby>けた<ruby>方<rt>ほう</rt></ruby>がいい。

Just so as to alert you, at night this area is dangerous and you had better be careful.

<ruby>簡単<rt>かんたん</rt></ruby>だが、お<ruby>礼<rt>れい</rt></ruby>まで(に)この<ruby>手紙<rt>てがみ</rt></ruby>を書くことにした。

It's nothing elaborate, but I decided to write this letter just to express my thanks.

<ruby>彼<rt>かれ</rt></ruby>が<ruby>困<rt>こま</rt></ruby>っているというから、<ruby>参考<rt>さんこう</rt></ruby>まで(に)ノートを<ruby>貸<rt>か</rt></ruby>してやったがあれから<ruby>何<rt>なに</rt></ruby>も言ってこない。

He said he was having problems, and I lent him my notes just so he'd have something to refer to. That was the last I heard from him.

---

(4)

> no need to; not necessary to
> Similar to: *hitsuyō ga nai*
>
> V *made mo naku*
> No need to V.
>
> See also: **iu made mo nai**

言うまでもなく、日本は島国である。

Needless to say, Japan is an island country.

こんな<ruby>簡単<rt>かんたん</rt></ruby>なことは<ruby>説明<rt>せつめい</rt></ruby>するまでもなく、<ruby>分<rt>わ</rt></ruby>かるはずである。

Such simple matters I expect you will understand without any need to have them explained.

made da までだ See **made (no koto) da**

made mo までも See **to (wa) iwanu made mo**

made (no koto) da まで(のこと)だ

> only; merely; just
>
> X *wa* Y *made (no koto) da*
> The explanation or reason for X is based solely on Y. The
> expression conveys emphatically that X does not go beyond Y or
> include anything else.

日本へ行ったのは柔道を習うために行った<u>まで(のこと)</u>で、別に
日本に住んでみたかったからだというわけではない。

I went to Japan to learn judo and for that alone; it was not because I
particularly wanted to live in Japan.

田中さんは信頼出来ない人だからあまり親しくしない方がいいと
言ったのは、君の将来を心配するからこそ、言った<u>まで(のこと)</u>
<u>である</u>。

When I told you that Tanaka was not a person to be trusted and that you
had better not get too close to him, I said that for one reason and one
reason only: I worry about your future.

-mai -まい

A classical negative suffix added to the citation form of U-group verbs and to either the stem or the citation form of RU-group verbs. In the case of *suru*, it follows either *suru, su* or *shi*. With *kuru*, it follows either *ko* or *kuru*.

(1)	will not; absolutely no intention Similar to: *tsumori wa nai* V-*mai* No intention to V.

ダイエット<ruby>中<rt>ちゅう</rt></ruby>は<ruby>甘<rt>あま</rt></ruby>いものは<ruby>絶対<rt>ぜったい</rt></ruby>に食べる<u>まい</u>と思うのだが、つい、食べてしまう。

When I am on a diet, I am determined not to eat sweets, but I end up eating them anyway.

人のうわさは気にす<u>まい</u>と思うのだが、<ruby>悪<rt>わる</rt></ruby>いことを言われるとやはり気になる。

I have no intention of worrying about gossip, but when bad things are said, it really bothers me.

(2)	probably not Similar to: *-nai darō* V-*mai* Probably not V.

<ruby>赤沢<rt>あかさわ</rt></ruby>さんは<ruby>病気<rt>びょうき</rt></ruby>なので、<ruby>今日<rt>きょう</rt></ruby>は<ruby>会社<rt>かいしゃ</rt></ruby>に<ruby>来<rt>く</rt></ruby>る<u>まい</u>。

Akazawa is sick, so s/he probably won't come to work today.

この<ruby>辺<rt>へん</rt></ruby>には<ruby>日曜日<rt>にちようび</rt></ruby>に<ruby>開<rt>あ</rt></ruby>いているデパートなどある<u>まい</u>。

In this area there probably aren't any department stores that are open on Sunday.

-mai ka -まいか See de wa arumai ka

-mai ka to -まいかと

> fearing that . . . may; concerned that . . . may
> Similar to: *-nai darō ka to*
>
> V-*mai ka to*
> Fearing that V may be the case; concerned that V may be the case.
>
> See also: **de wa arumai ka**; **wa shimai**

<ruby>今日<rt>きょう</rt></ruby>は日曜日でゆっくり<ruby>寝<rt>ね</rt></ruby>ていたいのだが、<ruby>夫<rt>おっと</rt></ruby>の<ruby>母<rt>はは</rt></ruby>が<ruby>急<rt>きゅう</rt></ruby>に<ruby>来<rt>き</rt></ruby>はし<u>まいかと</u><ruby>気<rt>き</rt></ruby>になっている。

Today is Sunday and I want to sleep late, but I'm worried that my husband's mother may drop in unannounced.

<ruby>鈴木<rt>すずき</rt></ruby>さんを<ruby>駅<rt>えき</rt></ruby>まで<ruby>迎<rt>むか</rt></ruby>えに行くことになっているが、<ruby>今朝<rt>けさ</rt></ruby>の<ruby>地震<rt>じしん</rt></ruby>で<ruby>新幹線<rt>しんかんせん</rt></ruby>が<ruby>動<rt>うご</rt></ruby>かなくなってしまったのではある<u>まいかと</u>駅に電話をかけてみた。

It has been arranged for me to pick up Suzuki at the station, but fearing that the bullet train may have halted service because of this morning's earthquake, I called the station to check.

mama　まま

(1) | as it is; as it was
A situation continues without change; something is maintained as it was.

使った辞書は本棚にかえさないで、その<u>まま</u>にしておいて欲しい。

Please don't put the dictionary that you used back on the bookshelf; I want it left right where it is.

日本ではオーバーを着た<u>まま</u>でよその家に入っては失礼である。

In Japan, it is rude to enter another's home while still wearing one's overcoat.

(2) | as one likes; whatever one pleases

いつか足の向く<u>まま</u>気の向く<u>まま</u>に旅行したいと思っている。

Someday I would really like to take a trip and go where I want whenever I want.

(3) | as; according to; conforming to requirements of the situation
Similar to: *tōri*

兵士たちは命ぜられる<u>まま</u>に戦地へと出かけて行った。

As ordered, the soldiers went off to the battlefield.

古本にしては高すぎると思ったが、どうしても欲しい本だったので言われる<u>まま</u>にお金を払った。

I thought it was too expensive for a used book, but because it was one I really wanted, I paid the price that was asked for it.

72

ma ni au　間に合う

Generally known in the sense of "be in time/be on time." There are other uses:

(1) | be of use
Similar to: *yakudatsu; yaku ni tatsu*

このコンピューターは随分古くなったが、ワープロとしてしか使
わないので、まだ<u>間に合う</u>。

This computer has become very out-of-date, but it is still useful because I
only use it for word processing.

この辞書は語彙数が少ないが日常会話用としては十分<u>間に合って</u>
いる</u>。

This dictionary has a limited number of words, but for use in daily
conversation it is entirely OK.

(2) | sufficient
Similar to: *tariru*

日本に一か月ほど行ってくるのには、贅沢をしなければ、五千ド
ルもあれば十分<u>間に合う</u>だろう。

Five thousand dollars ought to suffice for a month's trip to Japan,
provided that you are not extravagant.

家からの仕送りだけでは<u>間に合わない</u>ので、アルバイトをして金
を稼いでいる。

Because the money sent to me from home is not enough by itself, I have
a side job and am earning money.

masaka . . . -nai　まさか〜-ない

> certainly not; surely not
> Similar to: *sonna koto wa aru hazu ga nai*
>
> Expresses strong, emphatic negation and strong surprise or doubt.

あんなに親切な山本さんがまさかそんな意地悪なことをするはず
がない。

I cannot believe that one so kind as Yamamoto would do such a nasty thing.

あんまりいい顔色をしていなかったが、まさかそんなに大変な病
気だとは思わなかった。

S/He didn't look very well, but I certainly didn't think s/he was as ill as that.

mashite　まして

> to say nothing of; not to mention; all the more reason
> Similar to: *atarimae*; *issō*; *naosara*; *tōzen*
>
> See also: **iwan ya . . . ni oite o ya**

彼女は現代文学が分からない、まして古典が分かるはずがない。

She doesn't know modern literature—all the more reason why you can't
expect her to know the classics.

この本は大人でさえ難しい、まして子供に見せても無駄であろう。

This book is difficult even for adults—all the more reason why it's apt to
be useless to show it to children.

74

masumasu ますます

> more and more
> Similar to: *mae yori mo issō*
>
> An adverb that expresses a growing or intensifying degree of
> something. Often used with words that describe processes, such as
> *omoshiroku naru* (become interesting), *genki ni naru* (get healthy),
> *fueru* (increase), and *heru* (decrease).

アメリカのコンピューター<ruby>関係<rt>かんけい</rt></ruby>の<ruby>会社<rt>かいしゃ</rt></ruby>は<u>ますます</u>大きくなるばか

りである。

American computer companies are just getting bigger and bigger.

<ruby>現在<rt>げんざい</rt></ruby>の日本では、<ruby>従来<rt>じゅうらい</rt></ruby>どおりの<ruby>習慣<rt>しゅうかん</rt></ruby>に<ruby>従<rt>したが</rt></ruby>わない<ruby>若者<rt>わかもの</rt></ruby>が<u>ますます</u><ruby>増<rt>ふ</rt></ruby>

えてきていると言われている。

It is said that in present-day Japan, (the number of) young people who do
not follow the customs of old is increasing more and more.

mi 身　See **Appendix B** for a list of idioms and example sentences using **mi**

mireba みれば　See **ka to miru to**

miru to みると　See **ka to miru to**

mo ii ga . . . nara もいいが〜なら

X *mo ii ga . . .* X *nara* Y
It is all right to do X but if one were to do X, one would want to do it in a Y way. The writer approves of X, but gives certain conditions (Y) for X.

海外旅行をするの<u>もいいが</u>、する<u>なら</u>団体旅行ではいやだ。

Taking a trip abroad is all right, but if we do it, I am opposed to a package tour.

飲むの<u>もいいが</u>、飲む<u>なら</u>やはりさけが一番だ。

Drinking is all right with me, but as long as we are going to drink, sake is my choice.

mono もの

(1) V *mono*, where V can be positive or negative.
Used often to convey that something is common sense, customary, or natural. It is also used as an emphatic and exclamatory marker that expresses surprise in finding out some new information. For example, *"Osushi tte oishii mono nan desu ne"* suggests that the speaker didn't know that sushi was good, but now that s/he has tasted it, s/he realizes for the first time how great it is.

See also: **mono de wa nai**

そんな縁起の悪いことは結婚式の席上では口にしない<u>もの</u>である。

It is common sense not to utter such inauspicious comments at a wedding ceremony.

納豆はこんな味がする<u>もの</u>だとは知らなかった。

I didn't know *nattō* tasted like this!

(2) | N *mono*
Things pertaining to N, such as *otokomono* (things for men) or *yomimono* (things to read).

<ruby>最近<rt>さいきん</rt></ruby>は<ruby>男<rt></rt></ruby>ものか<ruby>女<rt></rt></ruby>ものか<ruby>分<rt>わ</rt></ruby>からないデザインの<ruby>服<rt>ふく</rt></ruby>が<ruby>多<rt>おお</rt></ruby>い。

Recently there are many clothes of a design that makes it hard to tell if they are for men or women.

<ruby>子供用<rt>こどもよう</rt></ruby>の<ruby>読<rt>よ</rt></ruby>みものとしては、この本は<ruby>適切<rt>てきせつ</rt></ruby>ではない。

This book is not appropriate as reading matter for children.

<ruby>西鶴<rt>さいかく</rt></ruby>の<ruby>作品<rt>さくひん</rt></ruby>は、<ruby>好色<rt>こうしょく</rt></ruby>ものよりも<ruby>世話<rt>せわ</rt></ruby>もののほうがおもしろいのではあるまいか。

Don't you think that among Saikaku's works his dramas of everyday life are more interesting than his erotic works?

(3) | V-*ta mono da*
Used in fondly recalling or remembering something that happened in the past.
Implies nostalgia over what used to be.

<ruby>若<rt>わか</rt></ruby>い<ruby>頃<rt>ころ</rt></ruby>はよく<ruby>徹夜<rt>てつや</rt></ruby>でマージャンをしたものだ。

When I was young, I often used to play mahjong all night.

<ruby>子供<rt>こども</rt></ruby>の<ruby>頃<rt>ころ</rt></ruby>、よくあの川へ<ruby>行<rt>い</rt></ruby>って<ruby>遊<rt>あそ</rt></ruby>んだものである。

When I was a child, I often used to go to that river and play.

(4)
> V-*tai mono da*
> Expresses the writer's wish. V-*tai mono da* is stronger than V-*tai* alone.

早く卒業して仕事をしたい<u>もの</u>である。

I want to graduate early and go to work.

日本へ行って文楽を見たい<u>もの</u>だ。

I want to go to Japan and see puppet plays.

mono da kara　ものだから

> because; since
> Similar to: *kara*; *node*
>
> X *mono da kara* Y
> Because of X, then Y. The expression combines two sentences and gives X as the cause or reason for Y. It is similar to *no de* but somewhat stronger in terms of indicating a cause, reason, or excuse for Y. *Mon da kara* and *monde* are conversational forms of *mono da kara* and *mono de*.

その当時は非常に忙しかった<u>ものだから</u>、子供の教育のことなど考える暇もなかった。

Because I was extremely busy at that time, I had no time to think about things related to my child's education.

社長のことを批判した<u>ものだから</u>、解雇されてしまった。

I criticized the president, so I was fired.

78

mono de もので See mono da kara

mono de wa nai　ものではない

> (1)　X *mono de wa nai*
> The negative of *mono da*.
>
> See also: **mono (1)**

<ruby>校内<rt>こうない</rt></ruby>マラソンで<ruby>一番<rt>いちばん</rt></ruby>になったからといってそんなに<ruby>大<rt>おお</rt></ruby>きな<ruby>顔<rt>かお</rt></ruby>をす<u>る</u><ruby>速<rt>はや</rt></ruby>い<u>ものではない</u>。もっと<ruby>速<rt>はや</rt></ruby>い<ruby>人<rt></rt></ruby>がたくさんいるのだから。

Just because you came in first in the school marathon, you shouldn't boast like that. There are many who are faster than you.

> (2)　V-*ta mono de wa nai* is much stronger than the simple negative of V.

あの<ruby>記者<rt>きしゃ</rt></ruby>にかかると、<ruby>何<rt>なに</rt></ruby>を<ruby>書<rt>か</rt></ruby>かれるか<ruby>分<rt>わ</rt></ruby>かった<u>ものではない</u>。

When it comes to that reporter, there is no way to know what s/he will write about you.

> (3)　V-potential *mono de wa nai* is a very strong negation and suggests that V is impossible.

こんな<ruby>固<rt>かた</rt></ruby>いステーキなど<ruby>食<rt></rt></ruby>べられる<u>ものではない</u>。

There is no way that one can eat such a tough steak.

mono ka　ものか

(1)
> definitely not; absolutely not
> Similar to: *keshite . . . -nai*
>
> X *mono ka*
> A rhetorical question used when expressing a strong negative idea, opinion, or conviction.

あんな奴と口などきいてやる<u>ものか</u>。

Do you really expect me to speak to that kind of guy?

あの子が一時間もじっとしていられる<u>ものか</u>。

Do you really expect that child to sit still for an hour?

そんな些細なことで戦争になる<u>ものか</u>と思っていたのだが . . .

I never thought a war would start over such a trivial thing as that.

(2)
> I wonder what/how . . .
>
> Question word X *mono ka*, where X is often a verb in the past tense.
> Used when wondering what would be best in a given situation.

弟がクビになったことを母に何と知らせた<u>ものか</u>と迷っている。

I am at a loss as to how to tell Mother that my younger brother got fired.

天皇制を批判する記事を書かねばならぬが、どのように書いた<u>ものか</u>と思案中である。

I must write a critical article on the emperor system, and I am thinking over how to phrase it.

mono nara　ものなら

(1)
> X *mono nara* Y
> If X, then Y. X is often a verb in the potential form that expresses something that is difficult to achieve or carry out successfully. The writer's desire for the realization of X is expressed in Y. This is sometimes used for sarcasm.

彼女は一人で会議の準備をすると言っているが、やれる<u>ものなら</u>やってみるといい。

She says she'll do the preparations for the meeting by herself. Let her do them, if she thinks she can.

この問題は非常に難しい問題だと思うが、出来る<u>ものなら</u>、解いてほしい。

I think this problem is an extremely difficult one. I want you to solve it, if you think you can handle it.

(2)
> V-*ō/yō mono nara* Y
> If one were to (try to) V and if V were realized, the result Y would be unfavorable.

父はとても厳しく、愚痴でもこぼそう<u>ものなら</u>、殴られたものだ。

My father was very strict. Were I to complain, I'd be beaten.

日本の会社の面接では、非常に個人的なことも聞かれるが、アメリカでは、個人的なことを面接で聞こう<u>ものなら</u>、裁判沙汰になりかねないから、気をつけた方がいい。

At company interviews in Japan very personal things are asked, but if you try to ask about personal matters in America you can end up in a lawsuit, so you had better be careful.

<ruby>戦前<rt>せんぜん</rt></ruby>は<ruby>天皇<rt>てんのう</rt></ruby>の<ruby>悪口<rt>わるくち</rt></ruby>を言お<u>うものなら</u>、<ruby>大変<rt>たいへん</rt></ruby>なことになったものだ。

Before the war, if one said something bad about the emperor, there were serious consequences.

mono no　ものの

> although; in spite of
> Similar to: *keredo(mo)*; *no ni*
>
> X *mono no* Y
> In spite of X, Y follows. Y is usually unfavorable.

<ruby>今日中<rt>きょうじゅう</rt></ruby>にその<ruby>仕事<rt>しごと</rt></ruby>を<ruby>全部<rt>ぜんぶ</rt></ruby><ruby>終<rt>お</rt></ruby>わらせるとは言った<u>ものの</u>、<ruby>実<rt>じつ</rt></ruby>は<ruby>終<rt>お</rt></ruby>わるかどうか<ruby>心配<rt>しんぱい</rt></ruby>だ。

Although s/he said s/he would have all the work done by today, I'm worried about whether it will actually get done.

<ruby>山田<rt>やまだ</rt></ruby>さんは<ruby>知識<rt>ちしき</rt></ruby>だけはある<u>ものの</u>、<ruby>一般常識<rt>いっぱんじょうしき</rt></ruby>や<ruby>情操面<rt>じょうそうめん</rt></ruby>で<ruby>少々欠<rt>しょうしょうか</rt></ruby>けるところがあるようだ。

Although Yamada has the intellect, s/he seems to be slightly lacking in ordinary common sense and sensitivity.

mono o　ものを

> although; in spite of
> Similar to: *keredo(mo)*
>
> X *mono o* Y
> Although X, Y; in spite of X, Y occurs. X might have come to pass but it does not.
> Y expresses the writer's regrets over what might have been.

あと少し時間があったら満点がとれた<u>ものを</u>残念ながら九十点し

かとれなかった。

If I'd had a little more time, I could have gotten a hundred, but
unfortunately I could only manage a ninety.

病気にならなかったら、ヨーロッパに行けた<u>ものを</u>、ひどい熱で
二週間も寝込んでしまった。

If I hadn't gotten sick, I could have gone to Europe, but I ended up in bed
for two weeks with a bad fever.

mono to kimatte iru ものと決まっている

> it is decided; it is the practice or custom
>
> Expresses customary or regular practice. This expression suggests
> strongly that the practice is the result of a decision that, once made,
> has become a regular practice.
>
> See also: **koto ni natte iru**

お盆にはお墓参りに行く<u>ものと決まっている</u>。

During the Bon Festival, it is the practice to visit the graves of one's
ancestors.

日本でもアメリカでも、結婚式がすんだら新婚旅行に行く<u>ものと
決まっている</u>。

In both Japan and the United States, it is the practice to go on a
honeymoon trip after one's wedding ceremony.

mo shinai　もしない

> absolutely not; certainly not
>
> V-stem *mo shinai*
> A very strong negative.
>
> See also: **te i wa shinai; wa shinai**

<ruby>田中<rt>たなか</rt></ruby>さんはよく<ruby>知<rt>し</rt></ruby>り<u>もしない</u>ことについてペラペラしゃべるから
いやになる。

I am disgusted with Tanaka because s/he talks glibly of things s/he knows nothing about.

<ruby>彼女<rt>かのじょ</rt></ruby>の<ruby>苦労<rt>くろう</rt></ruby>が<ruby>分<rt>わ</rt></ruby>かり<u>もしない</u>くせに<ruby>口<rt>くち</rt></ruby>を<ruby>出<rt>だ</rt></ruby>すのは<ruby>慎<rt>つつし</rt></ruby>んだ<ruby>方<rt>ほう</rt></ruby>がいい。

Since you have no idea what she went through, you ought to keep your mouth shut.

motomoto　もともと

> originally; in the beginning
> Similar to: *ganrai*; *hajime kara*; *izen kara*; *mae kara*
>
> X *wa motomoto* Y, where X and Y are both nouns.
> X is originally Y.
> Should not be confused with *mottomo*.

あの<ruby>人<rt>ひと</rt></ruby>は<u>もともと</u><ruby>下品<rt>げひん</rt></ruby>な<ruby>人間<rt>にんげん</rt></ruby>なのだから、<ruby>今<rt>いま</rt></ruby>さら<ruby>上品<rt>じょうひん</rt></ruby>に<ruby>振<rt>ふ</rt></ruby>る<ruby>舞<rt>ま</rt></ruby>え
と<ruby>言<rt>い</rt></ruby>っても<ruby>無理<rt>むり</rt></ruby>なことである。

Because that person is vulgar by nature, it will do no good at this late date to tell him/her to behave in a refined manner.

豆<ruby>腐<rt>とうふ</rt></ruby>は<u>もともと</u>中国のものであると言われている。

It is said that tofu was originally a Chinese dish.

moto ni suru　もとにする

> based on
> Similar to: *motozuku*
>
> N *o moto ni suru*
> Based on N; taking N as the basis.
>
> See also: **ni suru**; **ni yotte (4)**

この<ruby>作品<rt>さくひん</rt></ruby>は<ruby>源氏物語<rt>げんじものがたり</rt></ruby>のある<ruby>部分<rt>ぶぶん</rt></ruby>を<u>もとにして</u><ruby>書<rt>か</rt></ruby>かれている。

This work was written on the basis of a certain section of *The Tale of Genji.*

<ruby>日米間<rt>にちべいかん</rt></ruby>の<ruby>貿易不均衡<rt>ぼうえきふきんこう</rt></ruby>が<ruby>問題<rt>もんだい</rt></ruby>になっているが、どの<ruby>数字<rt>すうじ</rt></ruby>を<u>もとにし</u>ているのか分からない。

The trade imbalance between the United States and Japan has become a problem, but I don't know upon what numbers this discussion is based.

moto yori　もとより

> originally; from the beginning
> Similar to: *hajime kara*; *izen kara*; *mae kara*
>
> Serves the same function as *motomoto* but is not generally used in conversation. Also, *moto yori* has connotations of "from a starting point onward," whereas *motomoto* points more directly at the starting point itself. *Moto yori* is favored in academic writing.

今回の不始末は<u>もとより</u>私一人の責任で、グリーン氏には何の
関係もないことである。

The recent mismanagement was my responsibility from the outset. It
does not involve Mr. Green in any way.

大学紛争のころストライキに参加したが、<u>もとより</u>学校を退学さ
せられても仕方がないという覚悟のうえであった。

During the period of university disturbances I participated in strikes,
prepared from the outset to accept expulsion from school.

motte　もって See **o motte**

motte ninjiru　もって任じる See **o motte ninjiru**

mottomo　もっとも[尤も]

(1)	understandable; reasonable Similar to: *atarimae*; *dōri ni atte iru*; *muri mo nai*; *tadashi* N *wa mottomo da* Used to confirm that N is understandable, reasonable, or a matter of course for the reasons given.

斉藤さんは全然勉強しなかったから、試験に落ちたのは<u>もっとも</u>だ。

Saitō didn't study at all, so naturally s/he failed the exam.

86

健康に留意しない山本さんが病気になってしまったのは<u>もっとも</u>

だと言えば<u>もっとも</u>だ。

It stands to reason that Yamamoto, who is not attentive to his/her health, became ill.

(2)

> to be sure; although; yet
> Similar to: *shikashi*; *sō wa iu mono no*; *tadashi*; *tokoro ga*
>
> X. *Mottomo* Y.
> Used as a connector to begin a new sentence Y that contradicts what came before in X.

日本には四季の変化がある。<u>もっとも</u>北海道や沖縄は少し異なるが。

In Japan there are four distinct seasons. To be sure, Hokkaidō and Okinawa are slightly different.

このクラスの学生は優秀である。<u>もっとも</u>山本さんだけは少し他の学生より成績がおちるが。

The students in this class are outstanding. To be sure, Yamamoto has a record that's a bit lower than the other students'.

N

nado　など

(1)

> X (Y, Z) *nado*, where X, Y, and Z are nouns.
> Things like X (Y, Z).

昨日、デパートへ行って傘<u>など</u>買って来た。

Yesterday I went to the department store and bought an umbrella and other things.

最近アメリカで、日本語、中国語、韓国語<u>など</u>を勉強する学生が増えている。

The number of students studying Japanese, Chinese, Korean, and such languages has been increasing in America recently.

(2)

> Similar to: *nante*
>
> X *nado*
> X is something that is unexpected, unfortunate, or not particularly highly valued.

この問題は数学専門の人が出来ないのだから、私<u>など</u>に出来るはずがない。

This problem cannot be solved by mathematicians, so there is no way someone like me can do it.

ドルの価値がこんなに下がる<u>など</u>、誰も思いもしなかったに違いない。

I am sure that no one could have imagined that the value of the dollar would have decreased so much.

大学を卒業するまで海外旅行<u>など</u>、考えもしなかった。

Until I graduated from college, I never even thought about things like traveling abroad.

nagara　ながら

The use of *nagara* in the pattern V-stem *nagara* X, meaning "doing X while simultaneously doing V," is well known. There are two additional uses of *nagara*:

(1)	even though; despite; while; although Similar to: *keredomo*; *no ni* X *nagara (mo)* Y Despite one's expectations for X, there is an unexpected and adverse result (Y). See also: **mono no**

<ruby>佐藤<rt>さとう</rt></ruby>さんは<ruby>手伝<rt>てつだ</rt></ruby>うと<ruby>約束<rt>やくそく</rt></ruby>しておき<u>ながら</u>、<ruby>約束<rt>やくそく</rt></ruby>の<ruby>時間<rt>じかん</rt></ruby>に<ruby>来<rt>こ</rt></ruby>なかった。

Although Satō promised to help, s/he didn't come at the appointed time.

<ruby>残念<rt>ざんねん</rt></ruby><u>ながら</u>、その<ruby>件<rt>けん</rt></ruby>に<ruby>関<rt>かん</rt></ruby>しては私は<ruby>何<rt>なに</rt></ruby>も<ruby>知<rt>し</rt></ruby>らない。

It is regrettable, but I don't know anything about that matter.

<ruby>彼<rt>かれ</rt></ruby>の病気は<ruby>少<rt>すこ</rt></ruby>しずつ<u>ながら</u>、よくなっている。

His health is improving, even if only bit by bit.

<ruby>我<rt>わ</rt></ruby>が<ruby>家<rt>や</rt></ruby>は<ruby>貧<rt>まず</rt></ruby>しい<u>ながら</u>も、<ruby>皆<rt>みな</rt></ruby><ruby>幸<rt>しあわ</rt></ruby>せに<ruby>暮<rt>く</rt></ruby>らしている。

Even though my family is poor, we all live happily.

<ruby>今度<rt>こんど</rt></ruby>の<ruby>台風<rt>たいふう</rt></ruby>は<ruby>小型<rt>こがた</rt></ruby><u>ながら</u>も、<ruby>大<rt>おお</rt></ruby>きな<ruby>被害<rt>ひがい</rt></ruby>が<ruby>出<rt>で</rt></ruby>た。

Even though the last typhoon was small, there was a lot of damage.

(2) | Similar to: *no mama; to kawaranai; to onaji*
X *nagara no* Y
Y is as it was when it was X. Thus, as seen in the examples, *mukashi nagara no* Y means "Y as it was long ago," and *umarenagara* means "at birth" or "by nature."

あの婦人の言葉には昔<u>ながら</u>の日本語の持つ特徴がみられる。

In that woman's language you can notice characteristics of Japanese as it was long ago.

彼女は生まれ<u>ながら</u>、天才である。

She is a natural-born genius.

nai koto wa nai　ないことはない　See **aru ni wa aru**

naishi　乃至

(1) | or
Similar to: *arui wa; mata wa*
X *naishi* Y
X or Y.

今晩、鹿児島の南、<u>乃至</u>南西から台風が上陸するということである。

The report is that the typhoon will hit from the south or southwest of Kagoshima tonight.

英国の君主制、<u>乃至</u>日本の天皇制が永久に続くとは限らない。

It is not necessarily the case that the British monarchy or the Japanese emperor system will last forever.

(2)

> from . . . to
> Similar to: X *kara* Y *made*
>
> X *naishi* Y
> From X to Y.

明日<u>乃至</u>明後日にかけて大雨注意報が出ている。
<ruby>明日<rt>みょうにち</rt></ruby> <ruby>明後日<rt>みょうごにち</rt></ruby> <ruby>大雨注意報<rt>おおあめちゅういほう</rt></ruby> <ruby>出<rt>で</rt></ruby>

There is a heavy rain warning extending from tomorrow until the day after tomorrow.

この会場には百人<u>乃至</u>百五十人、入れるはずである。
<ruby>会場<rt>かいじょう</rt></ruby> <ruby>入<rt>はい</rt></ruby>

I expect that anywhere from 100 to 150 people can fit inside this meeting hall.

-nai uchi ni   -ないうちに

> before
>
> V *nai uchi ni* X
> Before V, X. V represents something beyond the speaker's control.

子供が目を覚ま<u>さないうちに</u>新聞を読もう。
<ruby>子供<rt>こども</rt></ruby> <ruby>目<rt>め</rt></ruby> <ruby>覚<rt>さ</rt></ruby> <ruby>新聞<rt>しんぶん</rt></ruby>

Before my child wakes up, I'll read the paper.

雨が降ら<u>ないうちに</u>、買物に行って来よう。
<ruby>雨<rt>あめ</rt></ruby> <ruby>降<rt>ふ</rt></ruby> <ruby>買物<rt>かいもの</rt></ruby> <ruby>来<rt>こ</rt></ruby>

Before it starts raining, I'll go shopping.

naku なく See ni (mo) naku

namaji　なまじ

> not fully; not thoroughly; not completely
>
> An adverbial form that suggests that an action or state is incomplete or insufficient.
> *Namajii* is an alternate form of *namaji*. *Namajikka na* is used as a noun-modifying form.

外国の政策になまじ干渉などするものではない。

We should not interfere half-heartedly in the policies of other countries.

あの画家の絵は、なまじっかな金では手に入らない。

With a slim purse you won't get paintings by that artist.

なまじっかな知識は、むしろない方がいい。

A little knowledge is worse than none.

nami　並

> like; the same as
> Similar to: *to onaji yō*
>
> N *nami*
> Like N; the same as N.

出世しようと思うなら、人並のことをしていてはならない。もっと積極的にいろいろなことに参加すべきである。

If you are thinking of making it in the world, you can't be like everyone else. You have to get more actively involved in various things.

92

欧米人<u>並</u>の生活水準を達成するのがこの国の政府の目標であった。

Reaching a standard of living on a level with Europeans and Americans was this country's goal.

nanigoto da 何事だ See **to wa nanigoto da**

nante なんて See **nado (2)**

nanto . . . ka なんと〜か

> What (a) . . . !; How . . . !
>
> *Nanto* X *ka*
> Used when one wishes to emphasize how impressed one is with X.
> Often used in *nanto* X *darō/de arō ka* patterns.

京都には<u>なんと</u>静かな旅館が多いことであろう<u>か</u>。

In Kyoto there are so many quiet Japanese inns!

彼女は<u>なんと</u>おもしろい人物であろう<u>か</u>。

What an interesting person she is!

-naosu -直す

> V-stem-*naosu*
> Do V again and do it better.

答案を出す前にもう一度よく見<u>直す</u>べきである。

Before you hand in your exam, you should look it over carefully one more time.

源氏物語はむずかしいので、何度も読み<u>直した</u>方がいい。

Because *The Tale of Genji* is difficult, it is better to read it over many times.

この建物はずいぶん古くなったので、建て<u>直す</u>ことにした。

This building has become quite old, so we decided to renovate it.

nara de wa　ならでは

> X *wa* N *nara de wa*
> X is something that is made possible or has a particular quality because of N.

ホール氏の歴史書は外国人<u>ならでは</u>の視点に立った中世日本研究だと言われている。

They say that Hall's history book is a study of medieval Japan that was made possible only by his viewpoint as a foreigner.

こんなにたくさん寄付金が集まるのは、この大学<u>ならでは</u>のことであろう。

The amassing of such a huge endowment is unique to this college.

nareba　なれば　See　to naru to

-nareru -なれる［-慣れる］

> used to; accustomed to
>
> V-stem-*nareru*
> Get used to V; become accustomed to V.

ニューヨークに住み<u>慣れる</u>と小さな町の生活は退屈であろう。

After you get accustomed to living in New York, small-town life will likely be boring.

私はこの種類のコンピューターしか使い<u>慣れていない</u>ので、ほかのものは残念ながら使えないと思う。

Since I am only used to using this kind of computer, unfortunately I don't think I can use anything else.

nari なり

> (1) as soon as
>
> V *nari* X
> As soon as V, then X. X occurs right after V.
>
> See also: **ga hayai ka; ka to miru to; soba kara; totan (ni); ya ina ya**

山田さんは、弟さんが地震で亡くなったという知らせを聞く<u>なり</u>、泣き出してしまった。

As soon as he heard that his younger brother had died in an earthquake, he burst into tears.

佐藤さんはほんのちょっと酒を口にする<u>なり</u>、真っ赤になった。

As soon as Satō drank just a tiny bit of *sake* his/her face got red.

---

(2) | like; something like
X *nari*
Something like X. X is provided as an example of something for which there may be better choices.

See also: **demo; nari . . . nari; to demo**

テレビばかり見ていないで、散歩<u>なり</u>した方がいい。

Instead of just watching TV, it would be better to do something like taking a walk.

彼女は今回の転職について一人で決めてしまわないで、わたしにだけ<u>なり</u>相談してくれればよかったのであるが。

Instead of deciding about her recent change of job by herself, it would have been better if she had discussed it even with someone like myself.

---

(3) | N *wa* N *nari ni*, where the expression is used adverbially.
N *(ni) wa* N *nari no*, where the expression is used as a noun-modifier.
N proceeds or acts as is expected of or appropriate for it, where it can be a person, an organization, a country, and so on.

学校を辞めることにしたのは、私は私<u>なり</u>によく考えたあげくのことだ。

My decision to quit school came after thinking about it a lot in my own way.

子供には子供<u>なり</u>の考えがあるから、一概に無視するわけにはいかない。

Since children have their own ideas, you cannot very well ignore them completely.

国によっていろいろな習慣があるが、どんなにおかしくみえる習慣でもその国にはその国<u>なり</u>の理由があるはずだ。

From country to country, there are all kinds of customs. No matter how strange these customs may seem, one would expect each country to have its own unique reasons for them.

nari . . . nari　なり～なり

> Similar to: *demo . . . demo*
>
> X *nari* Y *nari*
> In contrast to *nari* (2) above, where the meaning of "something like" was applied to only one possibility, here it is applied to two. Thus, the meaning becomes "something like X or something like Y," where X and Y are suggested possibilities.
>
> See also: **nari (2)**

彼女は何もしないで酒ばかり飲んでいる。運動する<u>なり</u>、旅行する<u>なり</u>したらどうかと言ってやった。

She drinks all the time without doing anything. I suggested that she do something like exercising or traveling.

ここは夏は暑いから、海へ<u>なり</u>、山へ<u>なり</u>行った方がいい。

The summers here are hot, so it is better to go somewhere like the seaside or the mountains.

nari ni　なりに

> as
> Similar to: *tōri ni*
>
> V *nari ni*, where V is in the citation form.
> Implies dependence or reliance on the subject of V.

非常に熱が高く、医者の言う<u>なりに</u>すぐ入院することになった。

With a high fever I was immediately hospitalized, as the doctor had ordered.

父の死後、いくばくかの遺産を相続したが、お金のことなどどうでもよく、銀行マンの弟のする<u>なりに</u>任せておいたら、知らないうちに大金持ちになってしまった。

Following the death of my father, I was left a modest inheritance. Not being concerned about monetary matters, I left it to my younger brother who is a banker to manage for me, and before I knew it I was very wealthy.

naru　なる

> Similar to: *to iu*
>
> N *naru*, where N is a noun modifier that represents hearsay.

ギリシァ人の家族が近くに越してきて、ギリシァ語<u>なる</u>ものを耳にしたが何を言っているのか全然わからなかった。

A Greek family moved into the neighborhood. I heard them speak a language that was supposedly Greek, but I didn't understand what they were saying at all.

私は生まれおちるや否や、祖父母のもとにおくられたため、初め
て母<u>なる</u>人にめぐりあったのは、小学校に入るころであった。

The moment I was born I was put in the care of my grandparents. For
that reason it was not until I entered elementary school that I met the
person who, I was told, was my mother.

naru mai ka　なるまいか　See **-te wa naru mai ka**

naru to　なると　See **to iu koto ni naru to**

naru to　なると　See **to naru to**

natte iku　なっていく

> X *natte iku*, where X can be N *ni*, or the *ku* form of an adjective.
> Unlike *natte shimau*, which suggests the completion of an event,
> *natte iku* emphasizes the process that ends up at X.

その店は初めは小さな店であったが、知らないうちにだんだん大
きなデパート<u>になっていった</u>。

That store was a small store at first, but before we knew it, it had
gradually grown into a large department store.

ここは辺鄙な田舎町であったが、交通の便がよくなるにしたがっ
て、日本でも有数の大都市<u>になっていった</u>。

This was a remote country town, but with improved transportation, it has
become one of Japan's great cities.

この大学の東アジア言語文化学部はまだまだ小さな学部である
が、だんだん大きく<u>なっていく</u>だろうと言われている。

The department of East Asian languages and cultures at this university is
still a small department, but they say it will probably continue gradually
to get bigger.

-neba naranu　-ねばならぬ

> must; have to
> Similar to: *nakereba naranai*
>
> V-*neba naranu*
> Must V; have to V.
> The classical form of *nakereba naranai*. With the irregular verb
> *suru*, the form is *seneba naranu*.

国と国との関係は、個人間の関係とは違った観点から測ら<u>ねばな</u>
<u>らぬ</u>。

You must assess relationships between countries from a different
perspective than that for relationships between individuals.

彼の話は誇張されがちであるから、注意せ<u>ねばならぬ</u>。

His statements are apt to be exaggerated, so you must be careful.

ni aran to　にあらんと

> try to be; intend to be
> Similar to: *de arō to*
>
> N *ni aran to* V
> Try to be N; intend to be N.
>
> See also: **de arō to suru; ō (1); ō to suru**

つね けんこう　　　　　　　ほっ もの　まいにちうんどう
常に健康にあらんと欲する者は、毎日運動すべきである。

People who want to be healthy all the time must exercise every day.

じぶん しんねん ちゅうじつ　　　　　　　　　　ただ　　　　けん かん
自分の信念に忠実にあらんとするならば、直ちにその件に関して
はんたいいけん
反対意見をのべなければならぬ。

If you are to be faithful to your own beliefs, you must express your

opposition to that situation right away.

ni atari　にあたり

> at the time of
>
> X *ni atari*, where X is a time, place, event, or action.
>
> See also: **ni saishite; ni tsuke(te); sai (ni)**

しどうしゃ かいこく　　　　　さんぴりょうろん わ
日本の指導者は開国にあたり、賛否両論に分かれた。

At the time when Japan was considering establishing relations with

Western countries, Japanese leaders split into pro and con groups.

101

山本先生のお宅を訪問する<u>にあたり</u>、何を持っていったらいいか
学生間で話し合った。

The students discussed among themselves what they should bring when
they visit Professor Yamamoto's home.

ni atatte　にあたって　See **ni atari**

ni atte　にあって

> in; at
> Similar to: *de*
>
> N *ni atte*
> Follows the time or place (N) where some action occurs.
>
> See also: **ni oite**; **ni okeru**

幕末の激動期<u>にあって</u>坂本龍馬は忘れてはならぬ人物である。

Sakamoto Ryōma was one of the unforgettable characters of the time of
upheaval that brought an end to the shogunate.

オランダ人は長崎<u>にあって</u>日本研究を怠らなかった。

The Dutch did not neglect to study about Japan (while they were) in
Nagasaki.

ni chigai nai　に違いない

> no mistake; no question; undoubtedly; without question
> Similar to: *ni sōi nai*
>
> X *ni chigai nai*
> X must be the case; X is certainly (surely) the case. Indicates emphatic belief by the writer that X is the case.

金魚が死んでしまった。水を長い間とりかえなかったからに違いない。

The goldfish have died. Without a doubt it was because their water wasn't changed for a long time.

あんなに人が並んでいるから、あの映画はおもしろいに違いない。

Because so many people are in line, that movie must be good.

ni fujiyū suru　に不自由する

> be in need of
>
> N *ni fujiyū suru*
> Be in need of N.

いいアルバイトをしているから小遣いには不自由しない。

I've got a good part-time job, so I don't lack spending money.

サンフランシスコは日本人が多いので、日本の食料品に関する限り、どんなものにも不自由しない。

In San Francisco there are many Japanese, so we don't feel any constraints with respect to Japanese food.

子供向<ruby>こどもむ</ruby>きの中国語の教科書<ruby>きょうかしょ</ruby>に不自由している。

We lack Chinese-language textbooks for children.

ni hoka naranai　にほかならない　See　hoka naranai

ni hoka naranu　にほかならぬ　See　hoka naranai

ni itaru to　に至ると

---

by; up to

N *ni itaru to*
When something reaches N; in reaching N.

徳川幕府<ruby>とくがわばくふ</ruby>も十九世紀半<ruby>せいきなか</ruby>ばに至ると、その勢力<ruby>せいりょく</ruby>は衰<ruby>おとろ</ruby>えた。

By the middle of the nineteenth century, the power of the Tokugawa shogunate had declined.

我<ruby>わ</ruby>が家<ruby>や</ruby>は十六世紀<ruby>せいき</ruby>から医師<ruby>いし</ruby>の家系<ruby>かけい</ruby>であるが、兄<ruby>あに</ruby>の代<ruby>だい</ruby>に至ると、開業医<ruby>かいぎょうい</ruby>ではなく、総合病院<ruby>そうごうびょういん</ruby>で働<ruby>はたら</ruby>くサラリーマンとなった。

My family have been physicians since the sixteenth century. In my older brother's time, instead of opening his own practice, he became a salaried employee at a general hospital.

ni itatte wa　に至っては　See　ni itaru to

ni kagirazu に限らず

> not only; not limited to
> Similar to: *dake de naku*
>
> N *ni kagirazu*
> Not limited to N; extends beyond N.
> The negative form of *ni kagitte* or *ni kagiri*.
>
> See also: **bakari de naku**; **bakari ka**; **ni todomarazu**; **nominarazu**

コンピューターは専門店<u>に限らず</u>、デパートでも売っている。

Computers are not limited to specialty stores but are sold at department stores as well.

このアパートは、学生<u>に限らず</u>、大学で仕事をしている人も借りることができる。

These apartments are not limited to students. Employees of the university can also rent them.

温情主義は日本<u>に限らず</u>、他のアジア諸国にもみられる。

Paternalism is not limited to Japan but can be found in other Asian countries as well.

ni kagiri に限り

> only; just
>
> N *ni kagiri*, where N is a noun.
> Limited to N; only N. *Ni kagiri* emphasizes N.
> *Ni kagitte* is sometimes used instead of *ni kagiri*.

この路線のバスはいつも時間通りに来るが、今日に限ってなかなかやって来ない。

On this line the bus usually comes on time, but today of all days, it simply won't come.

他の人ならともかく、あの親切な白石さんに限りそんな意地悪をするはずがない。

I don't know about others, but there's no way that that nice (person) Shiraishi could ever be so mean.

ni kagitte　に限って　See **ni kagiri**

ni kakaru　にかかる

> begin; start
> Similar to: *hajimeru*
>
> N *ni kakaru*
> Begin N; start N.

一休みしてからまた仕事にかからなくてはならない。

After the short break, we have to start working again.

締切りが近づいているから、原稿の仕上げにかかった方がいい。

Since the deadline is approaching, we had better get to the final draft of the manuscript.

ni kakawarazu　にかかわらず

> regardless of; irrespective of
> Similar to: *ni kankei naku*
>
> N *ni kakawarazu*
> Regardless of N; irrespective of N.
>
> See also: **towazu**

この学校には大きな体育館があるので、天候<u>にかかわらず</u>テニスの練習ができる。

Since there is a large gymnasium at this school, we can practice tennis regardless of the weather.

私はどうしてもインドに行ってみたいので、費用<u>にかかわらず</u>今度の団体旅行に参加するつもりだ。

I desperately want to go to India, and so I plan to join the next group tour regardless of cost.

ni kakete　にかけて

> (from) . . . to . . .
> Similar to: *(. . . kara) . . . made*
>
> X *kara* Y *ni kakete*, where X and Y are both nouns.
> From X (a noun of time or space) extending to Y (another noun of time or space).

今年の冬は厳しく、中西部から南部<u>にかけて</u>大雪が降った。

The winter this year has been severe, with heavy snowfall from the Midwest to the South.

この神社では、一日から三日<u>にかけて</u>新年の祝いの儀式が行われる。

At this shrine, ceremonies celebrating the New Year will be held from the first to the third.

ni kakete wa　にかけては

> with regard to; about
> Similar to: *ni kanshite wa; no koto ni tsuite ieba*
>
> N *ni kakete wa*
> In regard to N; with regard to N.

将棋<u>にかけては</u>、高橋さんに勝つ人はいないだろうと言われている。

When it comes to *shōgi*, they say no one can beat Takahashi.

日本語の文法<u>にかけては</u>、谷口先生ほど詳しい人は少ない。

When it comes to teaching Japanese grammar, few people are as knowledgeable as Professor Taniguchi.

ni kanshite　に関して

> about; with regard to
> Similar to: *ni tsuite*
>
> N *ni kanshite*
> About N; in regard to N; pertaining to N.
> A following particle *no* converts *ni kanshite* into a noun modifier with the same meaning as *ni kansuru*.
>
> See also: **ni kansuru**

日本の政治に関しては鈴木さんに聞くのが一番であろう。

Concerning Japanese politics, it is probably best to ask Suzuki.

この件に関して知っている限りのことを教えて欲しい。

I would like you to tell us everything you know concerning this situation.

日米間の貿易不均衡に関しての話はもう聞き飽きた。

I have grown tired of hearing about the trade imbalance between the United States and Japan.

ni kansuru に関する

> about; concerning
> Similar to: *ni kankei no aru; ni tsuite no*
>
> N *ni kansuru*
> About N; pertaining to N.
> The difference between *ni kanshite* and *ni kansuru* is not one of meaning but that the former functions adverbially and the latter as a noun modifier.

そのノーベル賞作家の幼年時代に関する記事を探している。

I am searching for articles pertaining to the childhood of that Nobel prize–winning author.

その言語学者の日本語に関する知識は稀にみるほどのものだ言っても言い過ぎではない。

It is no exaggeration to say that that linguist's knowledge regarding the Japanese language is virtually unique.

ni kimatte iru   に決まっている

(1)	a given; a matter of course
	Similar to: *kanarazu sō de aru*
	X *ni kimatte iru*
	X is always the case, fixed, a matter of course.

アラスカは寒い<u>に決まっている</u>。

It is a given that Alaska is cold.

子供はうるさい<u>に決まっている</u>。

Children are noisy by nature.

(2)	surely; undoubtedly
	X *ni kimatte iru*
	X must be the case. The writer strongly believes X to be the case. Not a fact of nature as in (1) above.
	See also: **ni chigai nai**

弟はサラリーマンだが、彼の読むものときたら、漫画か週刊誌くらいのもの<u>に決まっている</u>。

My younger brother is a white-collar worker, but when it comes to what he reads, you can bet it's comics or weekly magazines.

そんな安いテレビはすぐ故障する<u>に決まっている</u>。

Such a cheap TV will break down for sure.

ni kuraberu to   に比べると See **ni kurabete**

ni kurabete　に比べて

> compared to; in comparison with
>
> N *ni kurabete* X
> X in comparison to N.

京都の冬は東京に比べて寒さが厳しい。

Compared to Tokyo, Kyoto winters are much colder.

アメリカはほかの国に比べて移民の数がずっと多いのではないか
と思う。

I believe that compared to other countries, the number of immigrants in
America is much greater.

ni mo kakawarazu　にもかかわらず

> in spite of; despite
> Similar to: *no ni*; *keredo*
>
> X *ni mo kakawarazu*
> In spite of X; although X.
>
> See also: **kuse shite; no ni (1)**

彼は新しい車を持っているにもかかわらず、古いのばかり使って
いる。

Despite having a new car, he only drives his old one.

111

毎日漢字の勉強をした<u>にもかかわらず</u>、クイズで悪い点をとって
しまった。

Despite having studied *kanji* every day, I ended up with a bad grade on
the quiz.

彼女はひどい風邪<u>にもかかわらず</u>、仕事に出てくるから困ったも
のだ。

It's a problem because she comes to work even though she has a bad cold.

ni (mo) naku　に（も）なく

> N *ni (mo) naku* X
> X describes something that is unusual for N or unexpected from N.

今年は例年<u>に（も）なく</u>、雪が多いようだ。

This year there seems to be more snow than usual.

夕べは我<u>に（も）なく</u>、あんな失礼なことを言ってしまってすまな
かった。

I apologize for saying such rude things last night. It was not like me.

ni naru to　になると　See **to iu koto ni naru to**

ni natte iku　になっていく　See **natte iku**

ni oite において

> in; at
>
> N *ni oite*, where N can be a noun of time, place, or situation.
> In or at N.
> *Ni oite* is often used in written Japanese to indicate either *de* or *ni*.
> Can also be followed by the particle *no* to make a noun modifier.
>
> See also: **ni atte**; **ni okeru**

鎖国時代<u>において</u>、外国に開かれた窓は長崎のみであった。

During the period of seclusion, Nagasaki was the only window opened to the outside world.

戦後<u>において</u>、最も有名であった政治家の一人に吉田茂があげられる。

Yoshida Shigeru can be cited as one of the most famous politicians of the postwar period.

誰の人生<u>において</u>も、忘れられない出来事があるものだ。

In anyone's life there are unforgettable events.

当大学<u>において</u>の成績に関する方針は、ここ十数年変わっていない。

The grading policy at this university has not changed for the past ten years or so.

ni ōjite　に応じて

> in accordance with
> Similar to: *ni tomonatte; ni tsurete*
>
> N *ni ōjite* X
> X changes in response to or in accordance with N, where N
> represents a time or a situation.
>
> See also: **ni shitagai; ni tsure(te)**

あまり贅沢<ruby>贅沢<rt>ぜいたく</rt></ruby>をしないで、収入<ruby>収入<rt>しゅうにゅう</rt></ruby>に応じて生活<ruby>生活<rt>せいかつ</rt></ruby>をすべきである。

One should live in accordance with one's income and not be too
extravagant.

季節<ruby>季節<rt>きせつ</rt></ruby>の変化<ruby>変化<rt>へんか</rt></ruby>に応じて床<ruby>床<rt>とこ</rt></ruby>の間<ruby>間<rt>ま</rt></ruby>の掛<ruby>掛<rt>か</rt></ruby>け軸<ruby>軸<rt>じく</rt></ruby>をかえることにしている。

I make it a practice to change the scroll hanging in the alcove, following
the changes in the seasons.

ni okeru　における

> in; about; among; during
> Similar to: *de no; ni kansuru; ni tsuite no; no naka no*
>
> N *ni okeru*
> In, within, among, during N; or about, concerning N.
> Used particularly in written Japanese.
>
> See also: **ni atte; ni oite**

最近<ruby>最近<rt>さいきん</rt></ruby>小学校<ruby>小学校<rt></rt></ruby>における道徳教育<ruby>道徳教育<rt>どうとくきょういく</rt></ruby>が問題<ruby>問題<rt>もんだい</rt></ruby>になっている。

Moral education in elementary schools has become an issue recently.

私は文学作品<u>における</u>人間関係と現実社会の人間関係を比べた
論文を書いた。

I wrote an essay comparing human relations in literary works with real-world human relations.

ni oyobu　に及ぶ　See **oyobu**

ni saishite　に際して

> when; at the time of; on the occasion of
>
> X *ni saishite*
> At the time of X, where X represents either a time or a situation.
>
> See also: **ni atari; ni tsuke(te); sai (ni)**

来月、ベルリンにおいて国際会議が開催される<u>に際して</u>、日本か
らも代表がおくられることになった。

It has been arranged that when the international conference is convened next month in Berlin, representatives will be sent from Japan as well.

同窓会の発足<u>に際して</u>、学長に話をしてもらうことにした。

We decided to have the president give a talk at the time of the inauguration of the alumni association.

ni seyo . . . ni seyo　にせよ〜にせよ　See **ni shiro . . . ni shiro**

115

ni shiro　にしろ

> even if
>
> X *ni shiro*
> Even if X.
> The form derives from the classical imperative of *suru*. *Shiro* is
> seldom used as an imperative in modern Japanese—*shinasai* is
> more common. *Shiro* is, however, often used in the X *ni shiro*
> pattern to mean "even if." It is also often used in combination with
> interrogative words, as in the second and third examples below.
>
> See also: **ni shite mo (2)**; **tatoe . . . -te mo**

風邪で気分が悪いに<u>しろ</u>、あのオペラだけはのがさない方がいい。

Even if you are ill with a cold, you should at least not miss that opera.

あの学生はどんなに難しい問題に<u>しろ</u>、すぐ解いてしまう。

No matter how difficult the problem, that student solves it right away.

いくら田中先生が間違ったことを言ったに<u>しろ</u>、先生は先生であ
るから、悪口は慎んだ方がいい。

Even if Professor Tanaka said something that was wrong, a teacher is a
teacher so you had better refrain from speaking ill of him/her.

116

ni shiro . . . ni shiro　にしろ～にしろ

> whether . . . or . . .
> Similar to: *ni shite mo . . . ni shite mo*
>
> X *ni shiro*, Y *ni shiro*
> Whether X or Y. X and Y are cited as examples among possible others.
>
> See also: **to iwazu . . . to iwazu**

タクシーにしろ、バスにしろ、夕方は混むから早く行った方がいい。

Whether you go by taxi or by bus, it's crowded in the evening, so you had better go early.

大学院に行くにしろ、就職するにしろ、成績がよくなくては困る。

Whether you go to graduate school or seek employment, there will be problems if your grades aren't good.

ni shitagai　にしたがい〔に従い〕

> as; as a consequence
>
> X *ni shitagai* Y
> Y follows X either in temporal sequence or by cause and effect.
>
> See also: **ni ōjite; ni tsure(te)**

日米間の貿易の不均衡が大きくなるにしたがい、日本に市場を
開放させようとするアメリカの圧力もますます強くなっていった。

As the trade imbalance between Japan and America increased, American pressure to open markets in Japan became stronger and stronger.

日本語が上手になる<u>にしたがい</u>、日本人の友達も多くなった。

As his/her Japanese became proficient, his/her Japanese friends increased.

技術の発展<u>にしたがい</u>、数年前には夢のように思われていたことが現実となっている。

As a result of the development of technology, things that were considered dreams only a few years ago have become realities.

ni shitagatte　にしたがって　See **ni shitagai**

ni shita tokoro de　にしたところで

> even; even in the case of; even from the perspective of
> Similar to: *ni shite mo; no tachiba kara mite mo*
>
> N *ni shita tokoro de* X
> X is the case even from the perspective of N, where N is often a personal noun.
>
> See also: **ni shite mo (1)**

シカゴブルズ嫌いのトーマスさん<u>にしたところで</u>、マイケル・ジョーダンは有能な選手であると認めざるをえないだろう。

Even a Chicago Bulls hater like Thomas has to admit that Michael Jordan is a great player.

事実を知らされていなかった国民<u>にしたところ</u>で、昭和二十年の
戦局は敗戦を予測させるものであった。

Even from the perspective of the people, who were kept from knowing the
facts, it could be foreseen from the situation in 1945 that the war was lost.

ni shite にして

(1)

at
Similar to: *de*

N *ni shite*
At N. Used in the manner of the particle *de* to indicate time or
period.

吾、十五<u>にして</u>学に志し、三十<u>にして</u>立つ。

At the age of fifteen, I began learning; at thirty, I stood on my own.

彼は若年<u>にして</u>大会社の社長になった人である。

He is one who became president of a large company at a young age.

(2)

and; being
Similar to: *de*

N *ni shite*
Being N. Used similarly to the gerund form of the copula *de*.

コンピューターとは便利<u>にして</u>非常に役に立つものである。

Computers are convenient and very useful things

日本びいきのスミスさん<u>にして</u>我慢^{がまん}できないことは友達^{ともだち}にさえ
外人^{がいじん}と呼^よばれることだ。

That which even a Japanophile like Smith cannot endure is being called
"foreigner" even by his/her friends.

---

(3) | even
Similar to: *de mo; de sae*

N *ni shite*
Even N.

See also: **ni shite mo**

バート・ランカスターがスタントマンを使^{つか}わなかったということ
は映画通^{えいがつう}の山本さん<u>にして</u>知らないことであった。

Something that even film expert Yamamoto didn't know was that Burt
Lancaster didn't use a stuntman.

---

(4) | particularly because of
Similar to: *da kara koso*

N *ni shite*
Particularly because of N.

今^{いま}<u>にして</u>思えば、学生時代^{じだい}が一番幸^{いちばんしあわ}せな時^{とき}だったのだと思う。

Because I am looking back from the present, I think that my time as a
student was the happiest period of my life.

この親^{おや}<u>にして</u>、この子^こあり。

Like parent, like child.

ni shite hajimete にして初めて

> only (when); not until
>
> N *ni shite hajimete* X
> X follows after N, and X (not N) is experienced for the first time.
>
> See also: **-te hajimete**

病気をした時にして初めて健康の有難さは痛感されるものだ。

Only when you get sick do you realize the blessings of good health.

私と同じような経験をした人にして初めて私の苦労が理解できる。

Only those who have had experiences similar to mine can understand what I suffered.

ni shite mireba にしてみれば

> for
> Similar to: *ni shite miru to; ni shite mite wa*
>
> N *ni shite mireba* X
> Looking at things from the point of view of N (a personal noun), X is the case; for N, X is the case.
>
> See also: **ni totte**

娘の結婚式なのだから、親にしてみれば、盛大に祝ってやりたいと思うのが普通である。

When it comes to their daughters' wedding ceremonies, parents for their part usually want to celebrate on a grand scale.

彼女<u>にしてみれ</u>ば、別に悪気があってそんなことを言ったのではなく、親切のつもりだったのだと思う。

On her part, I don't think that was said with any malice; it was meant to be kind.

ni shite miru to　にしてみると　See　**ni shite mireba**

ni shite mo　にしても

(1)	even Similar to: *de sae; de sura; to shite mo* N *ni shite mo* Even N. See also: **ni shita tokoro de**; **ni shite (3)**

今回の取り引きはすべてうまく行ったのであるから、あのうるさい社長<u>にしても</u>、あまり文句が言えないはずである。

This time the deal went ahead smoothly, and I expect that even that difficult-to-please CEO won't be able to complain much.

この件に関しては、担当者の私<u>にしても</u>承服し兼ねる点があったので、社長が反対したのは無理もない。

With regard to this matter, there were points that even I, as the person in charge, had a hard time accepting; so it is understandable that the boss was opposed to it.

122

(2) even for
Similar to: *de atte mo; ni shitatte*

X *ni shite mo* Y
Even for X, Y. Suggests that while hypothetically X could be a sufficient condition for Y, in fact what is expressed in Y goes beyond what could be expected given X.

See also: **ni shiro; tatoe . . . -te mo**

東京の一流ホテル<u>にしても</u>、あのホテルは高すぎる。

Even for a first-class Tokyo hotel, that hotel is too expensive.

十年以上勉強している<u>にしても</u>、彼の日本語は並はずれてうまい。

Even for one who has studied Japanese for more than ten years, his Japanese is extraordinarily good.

ni shite mo . . . ni shite mo   にしても～にしても See **ni shiro . . . ni shiro**

ni shite wa   にしては

for

X *ni shite wa* Y
Considering X, Y. Y is a statement or a judgment made with the qualifications or explanations indicated in X. Y usually expresses something contrary to what one might expect from X.

このホテルは東京のホテル<u>にしては</u>、安い。

For a Tokyo hotel, this one's cheap.

かれ
彼は日本語を十年以上勉強している<u>にしては</u>、日本語が下手である。

For one who has studied Japanese for more than ten years, his Japanese is poor.

ni suginai　に過ぎない

> no more than; merely
> Similar to: *tada sore dake de aru*
>
> X *ni suginai*
> No more than X; merely, just, only X.

せんじつ　　　　　　　　　　きゅうか　　　　しごと
先日パリへ行ったのは休暇ではなく、仕事で行った<u>に過ぎない</u>。

I went to Paris the other day—not for a vacation, just for business.

でじま　　　　じんこう　しま　　　　　　　　　　ばくまつ　　せいよう　たい
出島は小さな人工の島<u>に過ぎなかった</u>が、幕末まで西洋に対して
ひら　　　ひと　　まど
開かれたただ一つの窓であった。

Dejima was nothing more than a small island, but it was the only window opened to the West until the late Edo period.

ni suru　にする

> X *o* Y *ni suru*
> Make X into Y; regard X as Y.

なん　　　　　　　　　もんだい　　ひつよう
そんなに何でもないことを問題<u>にする</u>必要はない。

It is not necessary to make such an inconsequential thing into an issue.

叔父は仕事上の失敗を苦にして死んでしまった。

My uncle took his failure in the realm of business very seriously and died
from it.

この小説には日本人の日常生活を題材にした話がたくさんでている。

In this novel there are many stories that take up the daily lives of
Japanese as their subject matter.

ni taishite　に対して

(1)
> in contrast to
>
> N *ni taishite* X
> In contrast to N, X is the case.

日本においては、大学に入学するまでよく勉強するのに対して、
アメリカでは大学に入ってからよく勉強する。

In contrast to Japan, where one studies hard up to the point of university
entrance, in America one studies hard after entering the university.

戦前の子供たちは、片仮名、平仮名の順で文字を教わったのに対し
て、戦後の子供たちは、平仮名、片仮名の順で文字を習っている。

In contrast to before the war, when children were first taught *katakana*
and then *hiragana*, children after the war first learn *hiragana* and then
katakana.

(2) | on; for; to; regarding; in regard to

N *ni taishite* X
N is the object to which attention is directed. X simply states the situation. May also be used as a noun modifier when followed by the particle *no*, in which case it may be used interchangeably with *ni taisuru*.

See also: **ni taisuru**

アメリカ人は個人の自由というものに対して非常な価値をおく。

Americans place great value on individual freedom.

学生は大学に対して新しい要求を出した。

The students presented new demands to the university.

先日新聞に環境保護に関する記事を書いたところ、それに対しての投書が多く寄せられた。

When I wrote an article on environmental protection in the newspaper the other day, many comments were sent in about it.

ni taisuru   に対する

toward; to; against; about; vis-à-vis

N *ni taisuru* X
X is a noun modified by N *ni taisuru*. For example, *kodomo ni taisuru taido* means "attitude toward children," as in the first example below.
There is no suggestion of hostility or opposition as there is with *hansuru*.

See also: **ni taishite (2)**

126

高橋さんはいい人だが、彼の子供<u>に対する</u>態度は信じられないくらい厳しい。

Takahashi is a nice person, but his attitude toward his children is unbelievably strict.

日本人の政府<u>に対する</u>信頼は薄れてきていると言ってもいい。

It is fair to say that Japanese people's trust in their government has diminished.

ni tarinai　に足りない

> not worthwhile
>
> X *ni tarinai*
> Expresses something that has low value with respect to X; something not worth X.

彼はいつもとる<u>に足りない</u>ことばかり言っているから、彼の言うことはあまり気にしない方がいい。

Because he is always saying things not worth taking seriously, it's better not to pay much attention to what he says.

その件に関する彼女の意見は考慮(する)<u>に足りない</u>くらい馬鹿げている。

Her opinion about that matter is so ridiculous it's not worth considering.

nite　にて

A classical form of the particle *de*

---

(1) **N *nite***
In or at N. N refers to the place where an action occurs.

だいいっかい
第1回のオリンピックはギリシャ<u>にて</u>開催された。

The first Olympic Games were held in Greece.

---

(2) **N *nite***
At N. N sets a time limitation.

てんらんかい　みょうにち　　しゅうりょう
ピカソの展覧会は明日<u>にて</u>終了する。

The Picasso exhibition will end tomorrow.

へいじつ　　じ　へいてん　　　　　　　　　　　　　しゅうまつ
あのデパートは平日は六時<u>にて</u>閉店することになっているが週末
　　　　　あ
は八時まで開いている。

That department store closes on weekdays at six but is open on weekends until eight.

---

(3) **N *nite***
By means of N.

らいねん　　　　　　　　　　　てがみ　　し
田中さんは来年中国に行くことを手紙<u>にて</u>知らせてきた。

Tanaka informed us by mail that s/he would be going to China next year.

交通の便がよくなり、船<u>にて</u>二週間もかかったところを飛行機<u>にて</u>十時間あまりで旅行できるようになった。

With improvements in transportation, a trip that had taken as long as two weeks by boat came to be possible in ten hours by airplane.

---

(4)	N *nite* Because of N. N indicates a cause or a reason.

思いがけぬ高熱<u>にて</u>やむなく仕事を休むことになった。

Because of an unexpectedly high fever, I was unable to avoid staying home from work.

その当時は毎日の残業<u>にて</u>、帰りはたいてい夜の十時すぎであった。

Because in those days I worked overtime every day, it was usually after ten at night when I returned home.

ni todomarazu　にとどまらず

> not limited to; going beyond
>
> X *ni todomarazu*
> The positive form, X *ni todomaru*, indicates that something ends with or at X. The negative, X *ni todomarazu*, suggests that it goes beyond, extends further than X.
>
> See also: **bakari de naku; bakari ka; ni kagirazu; nominarazu**

ナポレオンの勢力はフランス<u>にとどまらず</u>、ヨーロッパ大陸各地へとひろまっていった。

Napoleon's influence did not stop at France, but extended to every area on the European continent.

彼の知識は専門の科学のみ<u>にとどまらず</u>、人文の分野でも第一
人者と言えるほどである。

His knowledge does not end with science, his specialty; he may be
considered a leading figure in the field of humanities as well.

ni totte　にとって

> for; from the standpoint of
> Similar to: *no tachiba kara*
>
> N *ni totte*
> From the standpoint of N; for N.
>
> See also: **ni shite mireba**

<u>私にとって</u>は、横田さんが来ようと来まいと関係のないことである。

For me, whether Yokota comes or not is of no concern.

この文章は日本語の一年生の学生<u>にとって</u>は難しいかもしれない
が、二年生の学生<u>にとって</u>はやさしいはずである。

This sentence may be difficult for students in first-year Japanese, but I
expect it is easy for second-year students.

ni tsuke . . . ni tsuke　につけ〜につけ

> whether (it's one thing or another)
>
> X *ni tsuke* . . . Y *ni tsuke*
> Whether it's X or Y, where X and Y are a pair.
>
> See also: **ni shiro . . . ni shiro**

喜びにつけ、悲しみにつけ、思い出すのは亡くなった母のことである。

Whether I am happy or sad, my thoughts are on my late mother.

日本に関するニュースをテレビで目にするにつけ、新聞で読むにつけ、日本も経済大国になったものだなとつくづく思う。

Whether I watch news about Japan on television or read it in the newspaper, I realize fully that Japan, too, has become an economic superpower.

ni tsuke(te) につけ（て）

> when
>
> X *ni tsuke(te)*
> When X; in response to X; corresponding to X, where X represents circumstances or time.
>
> See also: **ni atari**; **ni saishite**; **sai (ni)**

我が子の成長をみるにつけ（て）、亡くなった夫のことが思い出される。

As I watch my child growing up, I am reminded of my late husband.

何事につけ（て）反抗してくる息子をどのようにあつかったものかと困っている。

I am troubled as to how to deal with a son who opposes everything.

ni tsuki　につき

> (1) | because
> Similar to: *da kara; no de*
>
> N *ni tsuki*
> Because of N. Gives a reason or cause for N.

本日はとりこみ中<u>につき</u>、勝手ながら休業することにする。

Because of events beyond our control, we shall be closed today. Please pardon the inconvenience.

急病<u>につき</u>、明日の会議はとりやめさせていただく。

Because of a sudden illness, we would like to call off tomorrow's conference.

> (2) | about; concerning
> Similar to: *ni tsuite*
>
> X *ni tsuki*
> About X; concerning X.
> Used mainly in written Japanese, whereas *ni tsuite* may also be used in spoken Japanese. *Ni tsuki* generally follows nouns but may also follow verbs, in which case a nominalizer such as *koto* is implied, as in the third example below. In such cases, *ni tsuki* may also be interpreted as "because," as in (1) above.
>
> See also: **ni kanshite**

学校側は、授業料値上げ<u>につき</u>、学生の意見を聞いてみることにした。

The school decided to ask for student opinion concerning the rise in tuition.

視聴覚教材を教室内で使った場合の教育的効果<u>につき</u>、論文をまとめた。

I completed a paper about the educational results of using audiovisual teaching materials in the classroom.

環境汚染を扱った新講座が開講される<u>につき</u>、方々から問い合わせが殺到している。

Inquiries are coming in from all sides concerning the new course to be offered on environmental pollution.

(3)

> per
> Similar to: *atari*
>
> N *ni tsuki*
> Per N. Units or proportions per N, as in "per person" or "per household."

この大学にあっては、学生一人<u>につき</u>千ドルの援助金が州政府から扶助される。

At this university, financial aid of $1,000 per student is provided by the state government.

このデパートでは一日<u>につき</u>百ドルのアルバイト代がでる。

This department store pays $100 per day for part-time workers.

ni tsure(te)　につれ（て）〔に連れ（て）〕

> in accordance with, along with, as
> Similar to: *ni tomonatte*
>
> X *ni tsure(te)* Y
> Along with X, Y occurs.
>
> See also: **ni ōjite**; **ni shitagai**; **to tomo ni**

医学が発達するにつれ（て）、平均寿命が長くなっている。

As medical science advances, the average life expectancy continues to increase.

正月が近づくにつれ（て）、街がざわついてくる。

With the approach of New Year's, the town begins to stir.

ni wa　には　See koto ni (wa); no ni (2)

ni yorazu　によらず

> no matter; not only
>
> X *ni yorazu*
> Not only in X; not just with X; not limited to X.
> Also, often used with interrogatives such as *donna* X *ni yorazu* (whatever X), *nanigoto ni yorazu* (no matter what), *dokosoko ni yorazu* (no matter where), *darekare ni yorazu* (no matter who).

ジョーンズさんは日本のことに関する<ruby>講義<rt>こうぎ</rt></ruby>と<ruby>聞<rt>き</rt></ruby>くや、<ruby>何事<rt>なにごと</rt></ruby><u>によら</u>ず<ruby>出<rt>で</rt></ruby>かけて行く。

As soon as Jones hears of a lecture concerning Japan, s/he goes to it no matter what it is about.

<ruby>私立<rt>しりつ</rt></ruby>大学<u>によらず</u>、<ruby>昨今<rt>さっこん</rt></ruby>では<ruby>国立<rt>こくりつ</rt></ruby>大学でも<ruby>授業料<rt>じゅぎょうりょう</rt></ruby>の<ruby>値上<rt>ねあ</rt></ruby>げが<ruby>著<rt>いちじる</rt></ruby>しい。

The rise in tuition has been remarkable not just at private universities but at national universities as well recently.

ni yori　により　See　ni yotte

ni yoru　による

(1)	due to; because of (X *wa*) N *ni yoru* X (either stated or implied) is due to N; X is caused by N. See also: **ni yotte (1)**

<ruby>彼女<rt>かのじょ</rt></ruby>が<ruby>司法試験<rt>しほうしけん</rt></ruby>に<ruby>合格<rt>ごうかく</rt></ruby>したのは彼女の<ruby>努力<rt>どりょく</rt></ruby><u>による</u>ものである。

That she passed the bar exam is due to her effort alone.

<ruby>運動会<rt>うんどうかい</rt></ruby>が<ruby>中止<rt>ちゅうし</rt></ruby>になったのは<ruby>悪天候<rt>あくてんこう</rt></ruby><u>による</u>。

The sports day was canceled because of bad weather.

(2)

> depend upon
>
> (X *wa*) N *ni yoru*
> X (either stated or implied) depends upon N.
>
> See also: **ni yotte (2)**

こうりょう おお すく とし
降雨量が多いか少ないかは、年による。

Whether rainfall is light or heavy depends on the year.

かいしゃ きゅうりょう がく ねんれい
この会社では給料の額は年令によらない。

In this company the amount of one's salary does not depend upon one's age.

ni yoru to　によると

> according to
>
> N *ni yoru to* X . . . *sō da.*
> According to N, X is the case. N represents a source of
> information. *Sō da* indicates information reported from an outside
> source.

ことし なつ れいねん あつ
テレビのニュースによると、今年の夏は例年になく暑くなるそうだ。

According to the news on TV, the summer this year will be hotter than
usual.

おだ はなし ほんだ らいねん てんきん
小田さんの話によると、本田さんは来年ロンドンに転勤すること

になったそうだ。

According to Oda, it was arranged that next year Honda will transfer to
London.

136

ni yotte　によって

(1)

> because of
> Similar to: *no okage de; no sei de*
>
> N *ni yotte*
> Because of N.
> This meaning of *ni yotte* is similar to that of *ni yoru* (1), but *ni yotte* is used adverbially.

せんげつ　なだれ　　　　　　ひゃくにん　　　　　ししょうしゃ
先月の雪崩によって、百人あまりの死傷者がでた。

More than one hundred people died in the avalanche last month.

こうこう　こうちょう　　　　すいせん　　　　　　　　　　　　　はい
高校の校長先生の推薦によって、この大学に入ることができた。

I was able to get into this university thanks to the recommendation from my high school principal.

(2)

> depending upon
>
> N *ni yotte*
> Depending on N.
> This meaning of *ni yotte* is similar to that of *ni yoru* (2), but *ni yotte* is used adverbially.
>
> See also: **ni yoru (2)**

こううりょう　とし　　　ちが
降雨量は年によって違う。

The amount of rainfall varies depending upon the year.

かいしゃ　　きゅうりょう　がく　ねんれい　　　　　　き
この会社では給料の額は年令によって決められるのではない。

In this company salary is not determined by age.

チップをいくら払うかは客<u>によって</u>違う。

How big a tip is left differs according to the customer.

---

(3)

> through; by means of; via (agency)
> Similar to: *de*
>
> N *ni yotte*
> By means of N.

その事件に関しては、テレビのニュース<u>によって</u>、知った。

I learned about that incident through the news on TV.

そんな些細なことは裁判沙汰にするよりも話し合い<u>によって</u>、解決すべきだ。

You should resolve such trivial matters by talking them over rather than by a lawsuit.

---

(4)

> on the basis of
> Similar to: *ni motozuite*
>
> N *ni yotte*
> On the basis of N.
>
> See also: **moto ni suru**

本山さんは書評<u>によって</u>本を買うことにしている。

Motoyama makes it a practice to buy books on the basis of book reviews.

この大学では、両親の収入<u>によって</u>、学生の奨学金額が決められる。

At this university the size of a student's scholarship is determined on the basis of the parents' income.

138

no amari (ni)　のあまり（に） See **amari (ni)**

no de wa arumai ka　のではあるまいか See **de wa arumai ka**

no koto (de)　のこと（で）

> X *no koto (de)*
> *No koto de* adds emphasis to the adverb represented by X.

私はやっと<u>のこと（で）</u>、司法試験に合格することが出来た。

Finally, I was able to pass the bar exam.

ようやく<u>のこと（で）</u>覚えた暗号をどうしても思い出せない。

For the life of me, I can't recall the code that I had mastered with such effort.

nomi のみ

> only; just; merely
> Similar to: *bakari*; *dake*
>
> X *nomi*
> Only X; just X; merely X.
> *Nomi* emphasizes a limit, indicating that X is the only possibility. Similarly, *dake* also suggests extent or limit. *Bakari* comes from the word *hakari* (scales), and it indicates degree in comparison with other possibilities. *Nomi* is more of a written form than *dake* or *bakari*.

人はパン<u>のみ</u>にては生きられない。

"Man cannot live by bread alone."

先日ゴッホの展覧会に行った。あまりの素晴らしさに目を見張る<u>のみ</u>であった。

The other day I went to a Van Gogh exhibit. It was so wonderful that I could only gaze in awe.

娘は私と同じぐらい背が高いのに、大きい<u>のみ</u>でまだ子供である。

Although my daughter is as tall as I am, she's just (physically) big and is still (emotionally) a child.

nominarazu　のみならず

> not only . . . but also
> Similar to: *dake de naku; sono ue*
>
> X *nominarazu* Y
> Not only X but Y as well. Thus, both X and Y. Similar to *ni kagirazu* and *dake de naku* but slightly different from X *bakari ka* Y. With X *bakari ka* Y, Y is more important than X; in X *nominarazu* Y, X and Y are equally valued.
>
> See also: **bakari de naku; bakari ka; ni kagirazu; ni todomarazu**

学期末になると、学生<u>のみならず</u>教師も疲れてくるものだ。

By the end of the semester, it's not just the students but the teachers, too, who get tired.

彼は日本の政治経済に精通している<u>のみならず</u>、文学もよく知っ
ている。

He is not only familiar with Japanese politics and economics, but
literature, too.

あの学生は成績が抜群である<u>のみならず</u>、スポーツも万能である。

That student not only has the best grades but is also good at sports.

no ni　のに

(1)	despite; in spite of; although Similar to: *keredo(mo)* X *no ni* Y Y occurs in spite of or despite X. See also: **ni mo kakawarazu**

毎日漢字の練習をしている<u>のに</u>、なかなか覚えられない。

Although I practice Chinese characters every day, I can't remember them
easily.

この時計は非常に高かった<u>のに</u>、すぐ壊れてしまった。

In spite of its high price, this watch broke right away.

(2)	in order to V *(no) ni (wa)* X In order to do V, X is necessary or advisable. See also: **tame (ni) (1)**

ケーキを作る(の)には、粉やバターが必要である。

In order to make a cake, flour and butter are required.

その大学の入学試験に合格する(の)には、毎日十時間ぐらい勉強

しなければならぬ。

In order to pass the entrance exam for that university, you must study for about ten hours every day.

-nu   -ぬ

A classical form of the negative suffix, *-nai*. With the irregular verbs *suru* and *kuru*, the negative forms become *senu* and *konu*, respectively.

はっきりしないことは軽々しく口にせぬこと。

You should not speak lightly about things of which you are not certain.

彼についてよからぬうわさが広まっている。

Nasty rumors about him are spreading.

思わぬことで時間をとられ、帰りの電車に遅れてしまった。

My time was taken up unexpectedly, and I ended up being late for my train home.

O

-ō -う

V-*ō*/*yō*

Whether the verb ends in -*ō* or -*yō* depends on the type of verb. RU verbs: *taberu*, for example, becomes *tabeyō*. U verbs: *nomu*, for example, becomes *nomō*. Irregular verbs *suru* and *kuru* become *shiyō* and *koyō*, respectively. The popular form used for suggestion or invitation, as in *ikō* or *tabeyō*, is well known. In addition, this form is also used as follows:

(1)	intend to; plan to Similar to : *tsumori* V-*ō*/*yō* Intend to V.

今年こそ本を二冊ほど書こうと思っている。

This year I'm thinking of writing as many as two books.

宿題をしてしまってからテレビを見よう。

I'm going to watch TV after finishing my homework.

(2) | probably; perhaps
Similar to: *darō*

V-*ō*/*yō*
Perhaps V.
Usually appears in sentence-ending position. Often used in combination with the potential form of verbs. May also be used with adjectives such as *yokarō*.

See also: **de arō**; **-karō**

コンピューターなしの世界はもはや考えられないということができよう。

You can probably say that a world without computers is already inconceivable.

健康上、運動は不可欠であると言えよう。

You can probably say that exercise is indispensable from the standpoint of health.

o ba をば

An emphatic equivalent of particle *o*, *o ba* occurs frequently in classical Japanese. *Ba* is etymologically the particle *wa* but is pronounced *ba* following *o*. *O ba* generally follows nouns but may also follow verbs, in which case a nominalizer such as *koto* is implied.

今年の十一月に大統領選挙が行われるが大統領候補の不法移民に関する方針をば聞かずして投票はし兼ねる。

There will be a presidential election this November, but I will have a hard time voting without hearing the candidates' policies on illegal immigration first.

144

その当時アメリカの指導者たちは日本国民に無条件降伏<u>をば</u>押しつけるより外に戦争を終結させる途はないと考えた。

American leaders at that time thought that there was no other way to end the war than to impose unconditional surrender on the Japanese people.

その当時まだテレビが普及しておらず、日曜日に家族そろって映画に行く<u>をば</u>楽しみにしていたものである。

In those days TV was not widespread, and I used to look forward to going to a movie with my whole family on Sundays.

-ō de wa nai ka -うではないか

> Similar to: *-mashō; -ō*
>
> V-*ō/yō de wa nai ka*
> Invitation to others to V; seeking agreement to V.

もう一度日米間の問題をじっくり検討してみ<u>ようではないか</u>。

Why don't we carefully examine the problems between the United States and Japan once more?

そんなつまらないことをとりあげて問題にするのはやめ<u>ようではないか</u>。

Why don't we quit raising questions about such trifling matters?

-ō ga . . . -mai ga   -うが～ -まいが

> Similar to: *ni shiro . . . -nai ni shiro; -ō to . . . -mai to; -te mo . . .*
> *-nakute mo*
>
> X-*ō/yō ga* X-*mai ga*
> Whether or not you X. -*Ō/yō* represents the affirmative form of
> verbs in most cases; -*mai* is the negative form. Can also be used
> with adjectives and the copula, however.

貴方が行こ<u>うが</u>行く<u>まいが</u>、私は田中さんの結婚式に出席するつもりだ。

Whether or not you go to Tanaka's wedding, I plan to go.

総理大臣の名前など知ってい<u>ようが</u>い<u>まいが</u>、我々には関係のないことである。

Whether or not they know the prime minister's name is something that doesn't concern us.

今日の映画はおもしろか<u>ろうが</u>おもしろかる<u>まいが</u>授業の一環として見なくてはならない。

Whether today's film is interesting or not, I have to watch it as part of my class assignment.

146

-ō ga . . . -ō ga   -うが～-うが

> whether or not
> Similar to: *-ō/yō to . . . -ō/yō to*; *-te mo . . . -te mo*
>
> X-*ō/yō ga* . . . Y-*ō/yō ga*
> Whether X or Y, where X and Y are paired words and are usually verbs but can also be adjectives or the copula.
>
> See also: **de arō**; **-karō**; **ni shiro . . . ni shiro**; **-ō**

あなたが酒<ruby>酒<rt>さけ</rt></ruby>を飲<ruby>飲<rt></rt></ruby>も<u>うが</u>たばこを吸<ruby>吸<rt>す</rt></ruby>お<u>うが</u>私の知<ruby>知<rt>し</rt></ruby>ったことではないが、健康<ruby>健康<rt>けんこう</rt></ruby>だけには気をつけた方<ruby>方<rt>ほう</rt></ruby>がいい。

It's not my business whether you drink or smoke, but you should take care of your health.

中華料理<ruby>中華料理<rt>ちゅうかりょうり</rt></ruby>であろ<u>うが</u>和食<ruby>和食<rt>わしょく</rt></ruby>であろ<u>うが</u>、御飯<ruby>御飯<rt>ごはん</rt></ruby>さえあればたいていの日本人は満足<ruby>満足<rt>まんぞく</rt></ruby>するものだ。

Whether it is Chinese food or Japanese food, most Japanese will be satisfied as long as rice comes with it.

oite   おいて   See **ni oite**

ōjite   応じて   See **ni ōjite**

okage おかげ

---

due to; thanks to

X *okage*. When X is a noun, it is followed by the particle *no*.
Thanks to X.
X is usually a favorable situation.

See also: **sei**

私がシカゴ大学の大学院で勉強することが出来たのは両親のおか
げだ。

Thanks to my parents, I was able to study at the graduate school of the
University of Chicago.

今年から春休みが二週間に延びたおかげで、ゆっくり休むことが
出来た。

I was able to take a good rest thanks to the fact that from this year
onward spring break has been extended to two weeks.

okeru おける　See **ni okeru**

-ō koto nara -うことなら

---

if possible
Similar to: *dekiru koto nara*

V-*ō/yō koto nara* X
If V were possible, then X. Limited in usage to a very small
number of verbs.

See also: **-ō**

なろ<u>うことなら</u>、一日も早く仕事をやめてゆっくりしたいものである。

If it could be done, I'd like to quit work as soon as possible and take it easy.

でき<u>ようことなら</u>、今すぐにでも日本に行きたいと思うのであるが。

If it were possible, I'd like to go to Japan this moment.

-ō mono nara -うものなら See **mono nara (2)**

o motte をもって［を以て］

> in; at; on; because of
> Similar to: *de*
>
> N *o motte*
> Similar in usage to N *de*, where N is a cause, situation, or time. In the latter case, *o motte* indicates the time when something happened.

俊寛は謀反のかど<u>をもって</u>鬼界が島に流された。

Shunkan was exiled to the island of Kikaigashima on suspicion of treason.

１９８９年<u>をもって</u>昭和は終わりになった。

The Shōwa era ended in 1989.

149

o motte ninjiru　をもって任じる[を以て任じる]

> profess to be; lay claim to be
>
> N *o motte ninjiru*
> Profess to be N.
> N is something desirable and positive that one professes to be,
> thinks oneself to be, lays claim to be, and so forth, but which is not,
> in actuality, the case.

<ruby>中村<rt>なかむら</rt></ruby>さんはたいした<ruby>研究<rt>けんきゅう</rt></ruby>もしていないが、<ruby>学者<rt>がくしゃ</rt></ruby><u>をもって任じ</u>ている。

Nakamura has not done research of any importance but professes to be a
scholar.

あの<ruby>会社<rt>かいしゃ</rt></ruby>は<ruby>倒産<rt>とうさん</rt></ruby>しかけているにもかかわらず、この<ruby>国一<rt>くにいち</rt></ruby>の<ruby>大会社<rt>だいがいしゃ</rt></ruby>
<u>をもって任じ</u>ている。

That company lays claim to being the strongest business organization in
the country, although it is (actually) on the verge of bankruptcy.

onajiku　同じく　See to onajiku

o . . . ni suru　を〜にする　See ni suru

-ō to   -うと

---

no matter (how, what, who, when)
Similar to: *-te mo*

X *ō to*, where X is usually a verb but can also be an adjective stem
followed by *-karō*, as in the third example below.
Preceded by an interrogative word.

どんなに疲れて<u>いようと</u>、どんなに遠い所であ<u>ろうと</u>、彼は
彼女に頼まれればすぐにどこにでも出かけて行く。

No matter how tired he may be, no matter how distant the place, if asked
by her he will go anywhere right away.

あの人が何を飲も<u>うと</u>何を食べ<u>ようと</u>私の知ったことではない。

Whatever s/he may drink, whatever s/he may eat is not my concern.

お客に招かれた場合は、出された食事が如何にまず<u>かろうと</u>、食
べてしまう方がいい。

When you are invited as a guest, it is better to eat everything that is
served, no matter how bad it may be.

-ō to . . . -mai to   -うと～-まいと   See **-ō ga . . . -mai ga**

-ō to . . . -ō to   -うと～-うと   See **-ō ga . . . -ō ga**

-ō to shinai -うとしない

> V-*ō*/*yō to shinai*
> Subject of V is unwilling to do V; does not want under any
> circumstances to do V.
>
> See also: **-ō**

あの人は人の言うことを聞<u>こうとしない</u>から、いくら忠告しても
無駄である。

Since that person is not willing to listen to what other people say, no
matter how much one may advise him/her, it is all in vain.

姉はたばこは体に悪いと知りながらも、なかなかやめ<u>ようとしない</u>。

Even though she knows that smoking is bad for her health, my older
sister is unwilling to quit.

o tōshite を通して See **tsūjite**

-ō to suru -うとする

> (1) | try to; intend to
> |
> | V-*ō*/*yō to suru*
> | Try to V; intend to V, where the attempt is usually unsuccessful.
> |
> | See also: **de arō to suru**; **-ō (1)**

明治維新を題材にした歴史小説を書<u>こうとした</u>が、うまくいかな
かった。

I tried to write a historical novel with the Meiji Restoration as the subject
matter, but it didn't go well.

夕べ八時ごろ電話をかけ<u>ようとした</u>が、電話が故障していて連絡
できなかった。

I tried to call around eight o'clock last night, but the phone was out of
order and I couldn't get through.

(2)

> be about to
>
> V-*ō*/*yō to suru*
> Be about to V.
>
> See also: **-ō**

家を出<u>ようとした</u>時に電話がかかってきて、会議に遅れてしまった。

Just as I was about to leave home, the telephone rang, and I ended up
being late for the meeting.

テニスの試合が始ま<u>ろうとしている</u>ところへ大雨が降ってきた。

Just when the tennis match was about to start, it began to rain heavily.

o . . . to suru　をとする　See **ni suru**

o towazu　を問わず　See **towazu**

o tsūjite を通じて See **tsūjite**

o ya をや See **iwan ya . . . ni oite o ya**

oyobu 及ぶ

> reaching, extending to
>
> (X *wa*) Y *ni oyobu*, where X and Y are both nouns describing times, places, or situations.
> X extends to Y; X reaches as far as Y.
> *Ni* may be replaced by *made* or *ni made*.

<ruby>桜<rt>さくら</rt></ruby>が<ruby>満開<rt>まんかい</rt></ruby>になり、<ruby>昨日<rt>きのう</rt></ruby>は<ruby>最高<rt>さいこう</rt></ruby>の<ruby>人出<rt>ひとで</rt></ruby>となり、その<ruby>数<rt>かず</rt></ruby>は<ruby>数万<rt>すうまん</rt></ruby>に<u>及ん</u>だという。

The cherry blossoms are in full bloom, and yesterday there were the largest crowds of all. They say that the numbers reached into the tens of thousands.

テレビのニュースによると、<ruby>台風<rt>たいふう</rt></ruby>の<ruby>被害<rt>ひがい</rt></ruby>は<ruby>九州南端<rt>きゅうしゅうなんたん</rt></ruby>から<ruby>本州<rt>ほんしゅう</rt></ruby>にまで<u>及んだ</u>そうだ。

According to the news on TV, the typhoon damage extended from southern Kyūshū to Honshū.

o yoso ni をよそに See **yoso ni**

P

-ppanashi   -っぱなし

> Similar to: *mama*
>
> V-stem-*ppanashi*
> V continues as it was.
> The verb suffix *-ppanashi* is a form of the verb *hanasu* (to let go).

昨日はひどく疲れていて、電気をつけっぱなしで寝てしまった。

I was so tired last night I fell asleep with the lights still on.

ここ一週間彼女と毎日テニスをしているが、こう負けっぱなしで
は、やる気がしなくなる。

Every day this week I've been playing tennis with her, but because I keep
losing, I don't feel like playing anymore.

寮の部屋のドアを開けっぱなしにして大きな声で話していたとこ
ろ、隣から文句を言われた。

When I was talking in a loud voice with my dorm room door open, there
was a complaint from next door.

155

R

-ra -ら

> Similar to: *-tachi*
>
> N-*ra*
> A noun pluralizer such as *sorera* (those), *kodomora* (children).
> Often used with personal pronouns such as *warera* (we), *karera*
> (they). Can also be attached to a person's name such as *Satō-san-*
> *ra*, where it suggests "Satō and his/her crowd."

<ruby>彼<rt>かれ</rt></ruby>らによると<ruby>坂田<rt>さかた</rt></ruby>さんらは<ruby>今日<rt>きょう</rt></ruby>は<ruby>来<rt>こ</rt></ruby>ないそうだ。

According to them, Sakata and his/her group will not be coming today.

<ruby>子供<rt>こども</rt></ruby>らはその<ruby>人達<rt>ひとたち</rt></ruby>に<ruby>対<rt>たい</rt></ruby>してあらゆる<ruby>限<rt>かぎ</rt></ruby>りのいたずらをした。

The children played all kinds of pranks on those people.

rashii　らしい

> (1) | seems that; appears to be
> Similar to: *yō da*
>
> X *rashii*
> Seems to be X; is apparently X.
> A conjecture based on reliable information that the writer has heard
> or read but that is not firsthand information. Similar to *yō da*, but
> *yō da* is conjecture based on firsthand information, usually visible.

<ruby>明日<rt>あした</rt></ruby>もまた<ruby>雪<rt>ゆき</rt></ruby>が<ruby>降<rt>ふ</rt></ruby>るらしい。

It seems that it is going to snow tomorrow, too (according to the
information I have from news reports, etc.).

156

東京の冬はニューヨークの冬に比べてそれほど寒くない<u>らしい</u>。

Compared to winters in New York, winters in Tokyo are apparently not as cold (based on what I have read or heard).

---

(2) X *rashii* Y

Y has qualities appropriate to X or expected of X. X and Y may be the same word, as *otoko rashii otoko* (a man worthy of being described as a man, manly), *Nihonjin rashii Nihonjin* (a real Japanese). Or X and Y may be different, as *otoko rashii hito* (a manly person). X *rashiku nai* (without Y) can also be used, as seen in the second example below.

中村さんはお茶もお花も習字もなんでも日本的なことのよく出来る本当に日本人<u>らしい</u>日本人である。

Nakamura is a truly Japanese-like Japanese who can do all manner of Japanese things such as the tea ceremony, ikebana, calligraphy, and so on.

日本では大声で話すのは女<u>らしく</u>ないと考えられている。

In Japan, speaking in a loud voice is thought to be unladylike.

S

sae . . . -ba　さえ〜 -ば

> if only
>
> X *sae . . . -ba*
> If only X; X alone is sufficient and nothing else is necessary.
> When X is a verb, the pattern is V-stem *sae sureba*, as in the third
> example below.

明日のパーティーに、秋山さん<u>さえ</u>来てくれれ<u>ば</u>、他の人が来な

くてもいい。

If only Akiyama comes to tomorrow's party, it will be all right if no one

else shows up.

この仕事<u>さえ</u>してしまえ<u>ば</u>、あとはゆっくりできる。

If we can just finish this work, we can relax afterwards.

期末試験が終わり<u>さえ</u>すれ<u>ば</u>、映画に行ったり推理小説を読んだ

りすることが出来るのであるが。

If I just get through final exams, I can do such things as go to the movies

and read detective stories.

sae (mo)　さえ（も）

> even
> Similar to: *mo*
>
> X *sae (mo)*
> Even X.
>
> See also: **sura**

ジョンソンさんは外国^{がいこく}の話をよくするが、実はカナダ（に）さえ（も）行ったことがない。

Johnson is always talking about foreign countries, but actually s/he has never even been to Canada.

最近^{さいきん}はアメリカでも日本語を教^{おし}える大学が増^ふえ、中西部^{ちゅうせいぶ}の小さな大学（で）さえ、講座^{こうざ}を開^{ひら}いている。

Recently, the number of universities where Japanese is taught has increased in the United States as well. Classes are held even at small colleges in the Midwest.

sai (ni)　際（に）

> when; at the time when
> Similar to: *toki ni*
>
> X *(no) sai (ni)*, where *no* is used when X is a noun.
> At the time when one did or is going to do X.
>
> See also: **ni atari; ni saishite; ni tsuke(te)**

日本語の辞書がいるので、今度東京に行った<u>際(に)</u>買って来よう
と思っている。

I need a Japanese dictionary, so I am thinking of buying one the next
time I go to Tokyo.

私の大学の図書館には日本語の本がたくさんあるので、必要の<u>際
(に)</u>は遠慮なく知らせて欲しい。

My university's library has many Japanese books, so when you need one,
I hope you won't hesitate to let me know.

saishite 際して See **ni saishite**

sareneba naranai されねばならない See **-neba naranu**

-saru -さる[-去る]

> completely; to the end
> Similar to: *kanzen ni . . . suru; shite shimau*
>
> V-stem-*saru*
> V completely; V to the end.

小鳥がたくさん木の枝にとまっていたが、鉄砲の音がしたかとみ
ると、一斉に飛び<u>去って</u>しまった。

Many birds were perched on the tree branches, but as soon as the rifle
shots sounded, they all flew away.

彼女と私の間にはいろいろな誤解があったが、過ぎ去ったことは
過ぎ去ったこととして新しく出直すことにした。

She and I had had many misunderstandings, but we decided to start over
again, letting bygones be bygones.

sasu さす

> Derives from the classical form *sesasu* and is often used in place of
> the causative *saseru*.
> Can appear alone or attached as a suffix to the stem of a verb.

留守番を小さい子供にさすのはよくない。

It is not good to have a small child look after one's house while one is away.

子供が病気にならないように栄養のあるものを食べさすようにし
ている。

We are trying to make our child eat nutritious foods so that s/he does not
become ill.

-sei -せい[-性]

> N-*sei*
> A noun suffix that makes the noun abstract.
> "Unique" becomes "uniqueness" (*tokushu-sei*); "necessary"
> becomes "necessity" (*hitsuyō-sei*).

この仕事は将来性がないので、どうしようかと思案中である。

This work has no future, so I am in the midst of considering what to do.

やまだ
山田さんがやって来る可能性がないことはないが、あまりあてに
しない方がいい。

It's not that there's no possibility of Yamada's coming, but I wouldn't
depend too much on it.

sei　せい

> due to; because of
>
> X *sei*. When X is a noun, it is followed by the particle *no*.
> Due to X.
> X represents an unfavorable situation, and *sei* often places blame.
>
> See also:　**okage**

大久保さんが大事な会議に遅れたのは電車が来なかったせいで、
彼が悪いのではない。

Ōkubo's late arrival at the important meeting was because the train didn't
come. It wasn't his fault.

彼女は自分が落第したのは教師のせいだと言っている。

She says it is the teacher's fault that she failed.

seyo　せよ　See **ni shiro**

seyo ... seyo　せよ〜せよ　See **ni shiro ... ni shiro**

shika　しか

---

only; just
Similar to: *bakari; dake; nomi*

X *shika*
Only X; just X. Always followed by a negative expression.
The essential difference between X *shika nai* and X *dake aru* is that
in the former the lack of something is emphasized, and in the latter
the existence of something is emphasized.

このクラスでその漢字が読めるのはスミスさんしかいない。

In this class there is no one but Smith who can read those *kanji*.

この学校の日本語の授業では日本語しか使ってはいけないことに
なっている。

It's been arranged that in Japanese classes in this school you must use
Japanese only.

shimai　しまい　See wa shimai

shinai　しない　See mo shinai; wa shinai

shiro　しろ　See ni shiro

shitagai　したがい　See ni shitagai

shitagatte したがって See **ni shitagai**

shite して See **ni shite**; **-zu shite**

shite hajimete して初めて See **ni shite hajimete**

shite mireba してみれば See **ni shite mireba**

shite miru to してみると See **ni shite mireba**

shite mo しても See **ni shite mo**

shite mo . . . shite mo しても～しても See **ni shiro . . . ni shiro**

shite wa しては See **ni shite wa**

soba kara　そばから

no sooner than; immediately after
Similar to: *no sugu ato de; sugu ni; suru ka shinai ka no uchi ni*

V *soba kara*
Immediately following V.
Resembles *ya ina ya*, but whereas *ya ina ya* is used for onetime
occurrences, *soba kara* is used for frequent occurrences.

See also: **ga hayai ka**; **ka to miru to**; **nari (1)**; **ya ina ya**

学生というものは、習^{なら}うそばから忘^{わす}れてしまうものである。

Students are the type who forget things as soon as they learn them.

うちの子は片付^{かたづ}けるそばから散^ちらかしてしまうから困^{こま}ってしまう。

I'm upset because as soon as I straighten things up, my child messes
them up.

私は金遣^{かねづか}いが荒^{あら}いのか、稼^{かせ}ぐそばから遣^{つか}ってしまう。

Could it be that I'm a spendthrift? I spend money as soon as I earn it.

sō ka to itte　そうかと言って

however; even so; for all that
Similar to: *keredo(mo); shikashi*

X *sō ka to itte* Y
Having said X, one follows with Y, which contains information
that either qualifies or contradicts X. Y may be a new sentence, as
in the first example below.

親と暮らすのは面倒臭い。そうかと言って一人で暮らすのは金が
かかる。

It is a nuisance to live with one's parents. Even so, it is expensive to live
alone.

あの人は非常に頭がいいが、そうかと言って学校の成績が特別に
いいという訳ではない。

That person is very smart. Still, that does not mean that his/her school
grades are particularly good.

-sokonau　-損なう

> fail to; miss
>
> V-stem-*sokonau*
> Fail to V; miss V-ing.

今日はあまりの忙しさにお昼を食べ損なってしまった。

I was so busy today that I missed lunch.

いつも八時の電車に乗るのだが、今朝は少し寝坊をして乗り損
なった。

I usually take the eight-o'clock train, but I woke up a little late this
morning, so I missed it.

-sokoneru　-損ねる　See -sokonau

166

sono imi de その意味で

> in that sense
>
> X. *Sono imi de* Y
> X. In that sense Y. Y is taken into consideration with the limitations or information stated in X.

人文系の研究に対する政府の援助金が年々削減されている。<u>その意味で</u>今年、当大学が日本文化研究のために多額の援助を受けたということは注目されるべきである。

Financial support from the government for research in the humanities is decreasing year after year. In this context, special attention should be paid to the fact that this year our university received a large grant for research on Japanese culture.

近年、国民の政府に対する信頼は薄れてきている。<u>その意味で</u>、現総理大臣の国民の信頼回復への努力は高く評価されねばならぬ。

Recently, the people's trust in government has been undermined. In this context, the current prime minister's efforts to restore public trust must be highly regarded.

sore de ite それでいて

> even so; and yet; nevertheless
> Similar to: *sore na no ni*
>
> X *sore de ite* Y
> X and yet Y. Y does not reflect what one might have expected from what is known from X. *Sore de ite* may be used to begin a new sentence.

佐藤さんはクラスで一番成績が悪いが、<u>それでいて</u>、勉強しよう
としない。

Satō's grades are the worst in the class, and yet s/he doesn't try to study.

スミスさんは立派な体格をしている。<u>それでいて</u>、スポーツは全
くだめだ。

Smith has a great physique, and yet s/he is not good at sports at all.

sue (ni)　すえ(に)[末(に)]

> after; finally
>
> V-*ta sue (ni)*
> N *no sue (ni)*
> After V; after N.
> Compared with *ageku (no hate) (ni)*, where the result is always
> unfavorable, with *sue (ni)*, the result may or may not be
> unfavorable.
>
> See also: **ageku (no hate) (ni)**

彼は私のやり方に対して不平不満を述べた<u>すえ(に)</u>、部屋を出て
行った。

After expressing his dissatisfaction with the way I was doing things, he
left the room.

経済的な理由で大学を止めようと思っていたが、考慮の<u>すえ</u>
<u>(に)</u>、あと一年ほど頑張ってみることにした。

I was thinking about quitting school for financial reasons, but upon
consideration I decided to try and persevere for another year.

suginai 過ぎない See **ni suginai**

-sugi mo sezu ... -sugi mo sezu/shinai -過ぎもせず～-過ぎもせず／しない

> X *sugi mo sezu* Y *sugi mo sezu/shinai*
> Neither X nor Y. The *shinai* form may only be used in sentence-final position.

このアパートは大き過ぎもせず小さ過ぎもしない。学生のアパートとしては最適である。

This apartment is neither too large nor too small. As a student apartment, it is just perfect.

私の家は学校から遠過ぎもせず近過ぎもせず、便利である。

My house is convenient, being neither too far from nor too near school.

sumai すまい See **wa shimai**

sumaseru 済ませる See **sumasu**

sumasu 済ます

> make do with; get by with
>
> X *sumasu*.
> Make do with X; get by with X. When X is a verb, it is often in the
> negative form V-*nai de* or V-*zu ni*, as shown in the last example.
> In addition to the common meaning of *sumasu* (to finish
> something), there is another meaning that suggests "gettting by" or
> "managing" with something that is not the best possible choice.
> *Sumasu* is a causative form of *sumu* with the same meaning as
> *sumaseru*.
>
> See also: **sumu**

今日のお昼はホットドッグで済ました。

For today's lunch, I got by with a hotdog.

アルバイトの学生の面接は電話で済ますことにしよう。

Let's (decide to) take care of the part-time student help interviews over
the telephone.

風邪をひいて熱が出たが、薬を飲んで医者に行かずに済ました。

I caught a cold and had a fever, but I got by without going to the doctor
by taking some medicine.

sumu　済む

> make do with; get by with; manage with
>
> X *sumu*, where X may be an adjective, a verb gerund, or a noun
> followed by *de* or *dake de*.
> Make do with X. When X is negative, the form is either V-*nakute*
> or V-*naide*/V-*zu ni*.
> *Sumu* is an intransitive form that is similar in meaning to *sumasu*.
>
> See also: **sumasu**

夏は日が長いので、電気代が安くて済む。

Since the days are longer in summer, we get by with cheaper electric bills.

今年は収入が少ないので、去年ほど税金を払わなくて済むだろう。

This year my income has gone down, so I'm apt to get by with paying

less tax than last year.

スピード違反でつかまったが、幸いに警告だけで済んだ。

I was caught speeding but luckily got away with a warning.

sura　すら

> even
> Similar to: *mo; sae*
>
> X *sura*
> Even X.
>
> See also: **sae (mo)**

大学生（で）すら出来ない問題に中学生が答えることができた。

Junior high students were able to answer questions that even university students couldn't handle.

忙しくて新聞（で）すら読む時間がないのに、小説などとんでもない話である。

Novels are simply out of the question when I'm so busy I don't even have the time to read the newspaper.

sureba suru hodo　すればするほど　See -ba . . . hodo

suru　する　See ni suru

surumai　するまい　See wa shimai

suru to　すると　See to suru to

T

tabi ni　度に

> every time
> Similar to: *goto ni*
>
> X *(no) tabi ni* Y, where *no* is used when X is a noun.
> Every time X occurs. The emphasis is on frequency of occurrence of X.

ニューヨークに行く<u>度に</u>メトロポリタン美術館に行くことにしている。

Every time I go to New York, I make it a practice to go to the Metropolitan Museum.

山田さんの顔を見る<u>度に</u>早死にした山田さんのお姉さんのことが思い出されて仕方がない。

Every time I look at Yamada's face, I can't help recalling his/her older sister who died young.

食事の<u>度に</u>、手を洗った方がいい。

You had better wash your hands every time you eat.

tada . . . dake　ただ〜だけ

> only
> Similar to: *tada . . . bakari*
>
> *tada* X *dake*
> Only X; one only does X. Addition of *tada* adds emphasis.

あの学生は<u>ただ</u>いい成績をもらうこと<u>だけ</u>(を)考えて勉強している点取り虫である。

That student is a grind who studies thinking only of getting good grades.

竜巻後、残ったのは<u>ただ</u>地下室<u>だけ</u>であった。

The only thing left after the tornado was the basement.

私の会社の忘年会では、<u>ただ</u>飲んで騒ぐ<u>だけ</u>であるから、あまり行く気がしない。

All that's going to go on at my company's year-end party is drinking and lots of noise, so I don't feel much like going.

taishite　対して　See **ni taishite**

taisuru　対する　See **ni taisuru**

-taku   -たく

V-stem-*taku*

This form is well known in negatives of the desiderative (as in *tabetaku nai* or *ikitaku nai*), but it also has the following usages:

(1) | Equivalent of V-*te* form in the desiderative *(takute)*.

らいしゅう かいぎ　　　　　 し　　　　　　　　　　　　　 せきにんしゃ せき
来週の会議について知り<u>たく</u>、電話をしたが責任者が席をはずし

ていた。

Wishing to find out about the meeting next week, I telephoned, but the person responsible was not in.

かんきょうほご　　かん　　しょもつ こうにゅう　　　　ちか　　ほんや　　　　　　　　ざんねん
環境保護に関する書物を購入し<u>たく</u>、近くの本屋へ行ったが残念

ながらそれらしいものは何もなかった。

I wanted to buy a book about environmental protection and went to a nearby bookstore, but unfortunately nothing like that was available.

(2) | Equivalent of V-stem-t*ai to* when followed by *omou*, *zonjiru*, or the like.

しほうしけん ごうかく あかつき　　　　　 せ わ　　　　　　　 しょうたい　　れい もう
司法試験合格の暁には、お世話になった人々を招待してお礼を申

し上げ<u>たく</u>思っている。

On the occasion of passing the bar exam, I'd like to extend an invitation to the people who have helped me and to express my gratitude to them.

きゅうか　りよう　　　　　　　　　　おく　　ぶん
休暇を利用してできるだけ遅れた分をとりかえし<u>たく</u>思う。

By using my vacation time, I'd like to make up for the delay as much as possible.

175

tamaranai　たまらない

> cannot bear; cannot stand
> Similar to: *gaman dekinai*
>
> X-*te tamaranai*, where X is an adjective.
> N *de tamaranai*.
> Cannot stand X or N; cannot bear X or N.
> N represents nouns that express feelings, such as *shinpai* (worry), *fuan* (insecurity), *iya* (distaste), *kawaisō* (sympathy).

クーラーがこわれているので、暑くて<u>たまらない</u>。

The air conditioner is out of order, so the heat is unbearable.

今朝コーヒーを飲まなかったので、授業中に眠くて<u>たまらなかった</u>。

I didn't have any coffee this morning, so I was unbearably sleepy in class.

弟が試験に失敗したのではないかと心配で<u>たまらなかった</u>。

I was overcome with worry that my younger brother had failed the exam.

日本語の授業で人の前に出て会話の暗唱をさせられるのが嫌で<u>たまらなかった</u>。

I couldn't stand being made to get up in front of people and recite dialogues in Japanese class.

176

tame (ni) ため (に)

(1)	in order to; for the purpose of
	Similar to: *yō ni*
	V *tame (ni)*, where V is a nonpast verb.
	For the purpose of V; in order to V.
	See also: **no ni (2)**

やせる<u>ため(に)</u>甘_{あま}いものを食_すべ過ぎないようにしている。

In order to lose weight, I'm making it a practice not to eat too many sweets.

ジュリアードに入_{はい}る<u>ため(に)</u>、毎日_{まいにち}ピアノの練習_{れんしゅう}をしている。

In order to get into Juilliard, I practice the piano every day.

(2)	because
	Similar to: *kara; no de*
	X *tame (ni)*, where X is a verb or an adjective.
	Because of X.

夕べ雨_{ゆう あめ}が降_ふった<u>ため(に)</u>、野球_{やきゅう}の試合_{しあい}が中止_{ちゅうし}になった。

Because it rained last night, the baseball game was canceled.

気分_{きぶん}が悪_{わる}かった<u>ため(に)</u>、待望_{たいぼう}のコンサートに行くことができなかった。

Because I didn't feel well, I couldn't go to the concert that I had been eagerly anticipating.

この辺は一年中温暖である<u>ため(に)</u>、植物の種類が多く見られる。

Because it is warm all year round here, many varieties of plants can be seen.

---

(3) | N *no tame (ni)*
The context determines whether the meaning is "because" or "for the purpose of."

将来の<u>ため(に)</u>、貯金をしておいた方がいい。

One ought to put aside some savings for the future.

大雪の<u>ため(に)</u>、電車が遅れてしまった。

The train was late because of heavy snowfall.

-tari   -たり

X-*ri suru*, where X is the informal past (-*ta* form) of a verb, an adjective, or the copula.
Do things like X.
Often *nado* is added to suggest further that it is not just X but other things as well.

人のことばかりうらやましがっ<u>たり</u>しないで、自分のやるべきことをやるのがよい。

Rather than envying others and so forth, it's better just to stick to one's own business.

日本は二つに分かれて二つの国家ができ<u>たり</u>(など)することもなかったと考えられている。

Some think that Japan has never experienced anything like being divided in two with two distinct governments operating.

-tari . . . -tari　-たり〜-たり

> X-*ri* Y-*ri suru*, where X and Y are the informal past (-*ta* form) of
> verbs, adjectives, or the copula.
> Do things like X and Y, among other things.
> Where X and Y are opposites, the suggestion is that things keep on
> going back and forth between X and Y, as seen in the third and
> fourth examples below.

日本語はテープを聞い<u>たり</u>ビデオを見<u>たり</u>して勉強した。

I studied Japanese by doing things like listening to tapes and watching

television.

休みの日には、映画に行っ<u>たり</u>公園に散歩に行っ<u>たり</u>する。

On days off, I do things like going to the movies and walking in the park.

このところ、変な天気が続き、暑かっ<u>たり</u>寒かっ<u>たり</u>している。

In this area the unusual weather continues—sometimes hot, sometimes

cold.

子供らが部屋を出<u>たり</u>入っ<u>たり</u>しているので、この部屋はなかなか
暖かくならない。

Because the children keep going in and out, this room is not going to get

warm easily.

tarinai　足りない　See **ni tarinai**

-taru -たる

> Similar to: *de aru*
>
> N-*taru*
> A classical equivalent of *de aru*.

学生<u>たる</u>以上、毎日授業に出るべきである。
<ruby>以上<rt>いじょう</rt></ruby> <ruby>毎日授業<rt>まいにちじゅぎょう</rt></ruby> <ruby>出<rt>で</rt></ruby>

As long as one is a student, one should go to class every day.

古川さんは国文学者<u>たる</u>にもかかわらず、源氏物語を読んだことがないそうだ。
<ruby>古川<rt>ふるかわ</rt></ruby> <ruby>国文学者<rt>こくぶんがくしゃ</rt></ruby> <ruby>源氏物語<rt>げんじものがたり</rt></ruby> <ruby>読<rt>よ</rt></ruby>

I hear that Furukawa, despite being a Japanese literature specialist, has never read *The Tale of Genji*.

武士<u>たる</u>者は合戦の場においては一番槍を心掛けとすべし。
<ruby>武士<rt>ぶし</rt></ruby> <ruby>者<rt>もの</rt></ruby> <ruby>合戦<rt>かっせん</rt></ruby> <ruby>場<rt>ば</rt></ruby> <ruby>一番槍<rt>いちばんやり</rt></ruby> <ruby>心掛<rt>こころが</rt></ruby>

One who is a warrior must cherish the role of being first to attack the enemy on the field of battle.

-tashi -たし

> V-*tashi*
> A classical sentence-ending form that appears in letters and memos.
> It is used often in making requests and is the same as *-tai* in modern Japanese.

会議に間に合うよう、二時までにはおいでいただき<u>たし</u>。
<ruby>会議<rt>かいぎ</rt></ruby> <ruby>間<rt>ま</rt></ruby> <ruby>合<rt>あ</rt></ruby>

I would like you to come by two o'clock in order to be on time for the meeting.

このことは、くれぐれもお心にお留めいただきたし。

I earnestly beseech you to bear this matter in mind.

tatoe . . . -te mo　たとえ〜-ても

> even if; no matter how (with interrogatives)
> Similar to: *kari ni . . . to shite mo; moshi . . . da to shite mo*
>
> *Tatoe X-te mo*, where X is a verb or adjective.
> *Tatoe X de mo*, where X is a noun.
> Even if X.
>
> See also: **ni shiro**; **ni shite mo (2)**; **tokoro de**

たとえ一億円もらっても、そんな危ない仕事はしたくない。

Even if I were to get a hundred million yen, I wouldn't want to do dangerous work like that.

たとえどんなことがあっても、私の考えは変わらない。

No matter what happens, my ideas won't change.

たとえどんなに忙しくても、新聞を読むくらいの時間はとっておくべきである。

No matter how busy you may be, you ought to set aside time at least to read the newspaper.

その考えにたとえ反対でも、みんなで決めたことであるから守らねばならない。

Even if you are opposed to the idea, you should support it because it was decided upon by everyone.

181

-te habakaranai -てはばからない See **habakaranai**

-te hajimete -て初めて

> V-*te hajimete* X
> It is only with or after V that X occurs or is experienced.
>
> See also: **ni shite hajimete**

病気になっ<u>て初めて</u>自分が随分無理な生活をしていたということに気がついた。

It is only when I became ill that I realized I had been leading an extremely dissolute life.

子をもっ<u>て初めて</u>親のありがたさが痛感されるとはよく言われることである。

It is often said that one learns to appreciate one's parents only after having a child of one's own.

-te hoshii -て欲しい

> want someone else to
> Similar to: *-te moraitai*
>
> V-*te hoshii*
> One wants someone else to do V. The someone may be identified by either *ga* or *ni*.
> *-Te hoshii* contrasts with the *-tai* or desiderative form of verbs, which express what one wants or wishes to do oneself.

大切な会議なので時間通りに来<u>て欲しい</u>と何度も言っておいた
が、何人かやはり遅れてきた。

I told them any number of times that I wanted them to come on time
because it was an important meeting, but some came late anyway.

家を出る時に父にビールを買ってき<u>て欲しい</u>と頼まれた。

As I was leaving the house, my father asked me to get him some beer.

-te irai -て以来 See **irai**

-te i wa shinai   -ていはしない

V-*te i wa shinai*
Absolutely not V.
A more emphatic form of *-te inai*.

See also: **wa shinai**

あの人は口先では親切そうなことを言うが、心の中では人のこと
なんか考え<u>ていはしない</u>。

That person says nice-sounding things, but at heart s/he doesn't have
any consideration for others at all.

市川さんは私に怒っているそうだが、彼女に怒られるようなこと
は何もし<u>ていはしない</u>。

I'm told that Ichikawa is angry with me, but I've done nothing at all
about which she could be angry.

-teki ni itte   -的に言って

> if
> Similar to: *moshi . . . tara*
>
> X-*te wa*, where X is a verb or adjective in the *-te* form.
> N-*de wa*
> If X; when X.

今、新しいイタリアの映画を見せているが、芸術<u>的に言って</u>あまり感心できない。

They are showing a new Italian movie now, but artistically speaking it doesn't appeal to me.

あの学校では授業中、学生は一切質問をしてはいけないことになっているそうだが、教育<u>的に言って</u>問題がある。

I'm told that students are not allowed to ask any questions at all in classes at that school. From an educational point of view, this is a problem.

-te mo   -ても   See tatoe . . . -te mo

ten de wa   点では   See to iu ten de wa

-te tamaranai   -てたまらない   See tamaranai

-te wa　-ては

(1)
> if
> Similar to: *moshi . . . tara*
>
> X-*te wa*, where X is a verb or adjective in the *-te* form.
> N *de wa*
> If X; when X.

そんなに小さな声で話し<u>ては</u>誰も聞こえない。

If you speak in that quiet a voice, no one can hear you.

この会話はやさしくないから、テープのスピードが早く<u>ては</u>わかりにくいだろう。

This conversation is not easy, so it'll probably be difficult to understand if the tape speed is fast.

この本は今売れっ子の作家の書いたものであるが、こうつまらなく<u>ては</u>あまり読む人がいないだろう。

This book is written by an author who is very popular right now, but if it is this boring, I suspect that there won't be many people who'll read it.

そんな失礼な話し方<u>では</u>、誰も雇ってくれないであろう。

If you speak so rudely, no one is likely to hire you.

(2)
> keep . . . ing and . . . ing
>
> V-*te wa* X
> Keep V-ing and X-ing.

木村さんは亡くなった子供のことを思い出して<u>ては</u>、泣いてばかり
いる。

Kimura keeps recalling the child who passed away, and crying.

あの子の両親は私の教え方が気にいらないらしい。電話をかけて
き<u>ては</u>、文句ばかり並べたてる。

It appears that that child's parents do not like the way I teach. They keep
calling and complaining.

あのバスケットボールのコーチは大きな声でどなっ<u>ては</u>、選手を
きたえようとするが、チームは負けてばかりいる。

That basketball coach keeps hollering and shouting and trying to train
his/her players, but the team keeps losing.

-te wa naru mai ka   -てはなるまいか

> perhaps one must; probably one ought to
> Similar to: *-te wa naranai darō ka*
>
> V-*te wa naru mai ka*, where V is in the negative *-te* form (*-nakute*)
> of a verb.
> Perhaps one ought to V.
> *-Mai* adds negative conjecture, making the meaning similar to the
> more familiar *-nakereba naranai darō*.

折角いとこが遊びに来るのだから、飛行場まで迎えに行かなく<u>て
はなるまいか</u>。

Because my cousin is coming all the way to see me, I guess I should go
to the airport to meet him/her.

186

山田教授の講演は退屈であるが、指導教官であるから出席しなく
てはなるまいか。

Professor Yamada's lectures are boring, but since s/he is my adviser, I
should probably attend.

-te yamanai -てやまない

> V-*te yamanai*
> One does not stop doing V; one keeps on doing V.

私は渡辺さんの成功を祈ってやまないものである。

I continually wish for Watanabe's success.

人が何と言おうと、私は夫の無実を信じてやまなかった。

Regardless of what people said, I kept on believing in my husband's
innocence.

to arō とあろう See **to (mo) arō**

to bakari ni とばかりに See **bakari ni (2)**

to demo とでも

---

something like

X *to demo*
Something like X.

See also: **demo**; **nari (2)**

<ruby>日米関係<rt>にちべいかんけい</rt></ruby>は<ruby>切<rt>き</rt></ruby>っても<ruby>切<rt>き</rt></ruby>れない<ruby>相互依存<rt>そうごいぞん</rt></ruby>の<ruby>夫婦<rt>ふうふ</rt></ruby>関係のようなものと<u>でも</u><ruby>考<rt>かんが</rt></ruby>えてもよい。

One might think of the U.S.-Japan relationship as something like the mutually dependent relationship of a husband and wife, inseparable even if tested severely.

日本のバーはサラリーマンに<ruby>対<rt>たい</rt></ruby>して<ruby>家庭以上<rt>かていいじょう</rt></ruby>の<ruby>憩<rt>いこ</rt></ruby>いの<ruby>場<rt>ば</rt></ruby>を<ruby>提供<rt>ていきょう</rt></ruby>してきた<u>とでも</u><ruby>言<rt>い</rt></ruby>えるであろう。

It can probably be said that bars in Japan have assumed a role somewhat akin to providing the Japanese business employee with a place to relax better than s/he can at home.

彼女は自分で出来ることでも何でも私に言いつける。お手伝い<u>とでも</u>思っているのであろうか。

She orders me to do even those things she can do by herself. She must think I am her maid (or something).

todomarazu とどまらず See **ni todomarazu**

to ieba　と言えば

> speaking of; concerning
> Similar to: *no koto ni tsuite iu to*
>
> X *to ieba*
> When it comes to X; concerning X; speaking of X.

ワイン<u>と言えば</u>、「フランス」と思う人が多^{おお}いにちがいない。

When you mention wine, most people will certainly think of France.

ロス<u>と言えば</u>、すぐに「危^{あぶ}ないところ」と多^{おお}くの日本人は考^{かんが}えて
しまう。

When the subject of Los Angeles comes up, most Japanese immediately
think "dangerous place."

to ieba . . . (da)　と言えば〜（だ）

> X *to ieba* X *(da)*, where *da* is used when X is a noun.
> Although strictly speaking X can be said to be X, yet it is not fully
> the case.

外国^{がいこく}で育^{そだ}った井上^{いのうえ}さんが外交官^{がいこうかん}になったというのは自然^{しぜん}（だ）<u>とい
えば自然だ</u>。

In some sense, it is natural that Inoue, who was brought up overseas,
became a diplomat.

189

日本人の中には仏壇の先祖に向かって報告し、それから教会へ
行って結婚式を挙げる人がいるというのは奇妙（だ）<u>といえば</u>奇妙
（なこと）<u>である</u>。

It may in some sense seem strange, but among Japanese there are those
who will face the household Buddhist altar to report to their ancestors
and then go to a church to have a (Christian) wedding ceremony.

日本人の私よりアメリカ人のスミスさんの方がおすしをよく食べ
る。おもしろい<u>と言えば</u>おもしろい。

Smith, who is an American, eats sushi more often than I who am
Japanese do. If you think about it, it's funny.

to ieba ieru　と言えば言える

> Strictly speaking, you can say . . .
> Similar to: *iō to omoeba iu koto ga dekiru*
>
> X *to ieba ieru*
> While you may say that X is the case, it is not definitively so and
> there are qualifications to the statement.

この教科書は大学生に適切であると<u>言えば言える</u>。しかしながら
少し文法の説明が長すぎる。

It can be claimed that this textbook is appropriate for university students.
However, the grammatical explanations are a bit too long.

入学試験は公平な制度だと<u>言えば言える</u>が、いろいろな問題がある。

Although you can say that the entrance exam system is a fair one, there
are many problems with it.

to iedomo　と言えども

> even if; although; while
> Similar to: *to itte mo*
>
> X *to iedomo*
> Even if one can say X, some qualification to it follows.

ボストンは大<ruby>都<rt>だい</rt></ruby><ruby>市<rt>とし</rt></ruby>である<u>と言えども</u>、ニューヨークに<ruby>比<rt>くら</rt></ruby>べると<ruby>地<rt>ち</rt></ruby>
<ruby>方<rt>ほう</rt></ruby>都市のようなものだと言ってもいい。

Although Boston is a large city, one may say that compared with New

York it is more like a provincial city.

<ruby>犬<rt>いぬ</rt></ruby>は<ruby>人間<rt>にんげん</rt></ruby>の<ruby>最良<rt>さいりょう</rt></ruby>の<ruby>友<rt>とも</rt></ruby><u>と言えども</u>、<ruby>獰猛<rt>どうもう</rt></ruby>な<ruby>動物<rt>どうぶつ</rt></ruby>に<ruby>一転<rt>いってん</rt></ruby>することがあ

るから気をつけるにこしたことはない。

While dogs are said to be "a man's best friend," they may suddenly turn into

wild animals, so nothing is more important than to be on one's guard.

to ittara nai　と言ったらない

> N *to ittara nai*
> There is nothing like N. Strong emphasis on what is said in N, a
> descriptive noun. Can be used for both favorable and unfavorable
> situations.

<ruby>彼<rt>かれ</rt></ruby>は<ruby>長<rt>なが</rt></ruby>い<ruby>間<rt>あいだ</rt></ruby>タイに<ruby>住<rt>す</rt></ruby>んでいただけあって、彼のタイ<ruby>語<rt>ご</rt></ruby>の<ruby>素晴<rt>すばら</rt></ruby>しさ

<u>と言ったらない</u>。

Because he lived in Thailand for a long time, the excellence of his Thai is

unparalleled.

大きな家に何日も一人で残されて、その心細さ<u>と言ったらなかった</u>。
<ruby>家<rt>いえ</rt></ruby> <ruby>何日<rt>なんにち</rt></ruby> <ruby>一人<rt>ひとり</rt></ruby> <ruby>残<rt>のこ</rt></ruby> <ruby>心細<rt>こころぼそ</rt></ruby>

There was nothing like the feeling of loneliness I had when left alone in a big house for many days.

to itta yō na mono　といったようなもの

> N *to itta yō na* X
> X is a person or thing that is something like N.
> N and X can be linked by *to iu* or *to itta*, but the usage of N *to iu* X is broader than that of N *to itta* X. Compare the following two sentences, for example:
>
> (a) 日本の伝統芸術には能<u>という</u>ものがある。
> (b) 日本の伝統芸術には能<u>といった</u>ものがある。
>
> In (a), the phrase simply means "the thing called Noh." In (b), Noh is just one of the traditional Japanese arts—there may be others. *To itta* is used when giving examples, kinds of things. The addition of *yō* makes the statement less definite.

うどんは日本のスパゲッティ<u>といったような</u>ものと言えるであろうか。

Udon is something like Japanese spaghetti, I suppose you might say.

私の両親は付き合いやすくて、いつでも気軽に電話をかけてもいい<u>といったような</u>人たちである。

My parents are easy to get along with. They are the kind of people with whom you can readily talk on the phone.

この<ruby>町<rt>まち</rt></ruby>は<ruby>田舎町<rt>いなかまち</rt></ruby>なので、二十四<ruby>時間<rt>じかん</rt></ruby>オープンしている<ruby>喫茶店<rt>きっさてん</rt></ruby><u>と</u><u>いったようなもの</u>はない。

This town is a country town, so there is nothing like an all-night coffee shop here.

to itte (mo) ii　と言って（も）いい

> X *to itte (mo) ii*
> It is all right to say X; you can say X.
> Makes any expression softer, less firm, less direct.

ロシアの<ruby>社会<rt>しゃかい</rt></ruby>にはまだまだ<ruby>昔<rt>むかし</rt></ruby>ながらの<ruby>悪習<rt>あくしゅう</rt></ruby>が<ruby>残<rt>のこ</rt></ruby>っている<u>と言って</u><u>（も）よい</u>。

One may say that bad customs of the past still remain in Russian society.

<ruby>今日<rt>こんにち</rt></ruby>のアメリカにおいては<ruby>多<rt>おお</rt></ruby>くの<ruby>人々<rt>ひとびと</rt></ruby>が<ruby>小型車<rt>こがたしゃ</rt></ruby>を<ruby>運転<rt>うんてん</rt></ruby>している<u>と</u><u>言って（も）いい</u>。

It is fair to say that in the United States of today many people are driving compact cars.

to itte (mo) ii kurai　と言って（も）いいくらい

> Similar to: *to itte (mo) ii hodo*
>
> X *to itte (mo) ii kurai*
> Although one cannot state that something is X, it is nearly equivalent to X.
>
> See also: **kurai**

スミスさんは日本人<u>と言って（も）いい</u>くらい<ruby>上手<rt>じょうず</rt></ruby>に日本語を<ruby>話<rt>はな</rt></ruby>す。

Smith speaks Japanese almost like a Japanese.

<ruby>田中<rt>たなか</rt></ruby>さんは<ruby>非常<rt>ひじょう</rt></ruby>に<ruby>早<rt>はや</rt></ruby>く<ruby>泳<rt>およ</rt></ruby>ぐことができる。オリンピックの<ruby>選手<rt>せんしゅ</rt></ruby>に

なれる<u>と言って（も）いい</u>くらいだ。

Tanaka can swim very fast. It's fair to say that s/he is of Olympic

caliber.

to itte (mo) yoi　と言って（も）よい　See to itte (mo) ii

to iu fū ni　という風に

Similar to: *to iu yō ni*

N *to iu fū ni*
In the way, manner of N.

アメリカの<ruby>多<rt>おお</rt></ruby>くの大学においては、九十点から百点まではＡ、八

十点から八十九点まではＢ、七十点から七十九点まではＣ<u>という</u>
<u><ruby>風<rt>せいせき</rt></ruby>に</u><ruby>成績<rt>せいせき</rt></ruby>の<ruby>基準<rt>きじゅん</rt></ruby>が<ruby>決<rt>き</rt></ruby>まっている。

At most universities in the United States, the standard for grades is set

out in this way: from 90 to 100 is an "A," from 80 to 89 is a "B," and

from 70 to 79 is a "C."

たいていの<ruby>劇場<rt>げきじょう</rt></ruby>では、<ruby>一番高<rt>いちばんたか</rt></ruby>い<ruby>席<rt>せき</rt></ruby>、<ruby>中<rt>ちゅう</rt></ruby>くらいの席、一番<ruby>安<rt>やす</rt></ruby>い席<u>と</u>
<u>いう風に</u><ruby>前<rt>まえ</rt></ruby>の<ruby>方<rt>ほう</rt></ruby>からそれぞれ<ruby>値段<rt>ねだん</rt></ruby>が<ruby>違<rt>ちが</rt></ruby>う。

At most theaters prices differ with distance from the front in the

following manner: most expensive, moderately expensive, and cheapest.

(to iu) hodo no ... nai　（という）ほどの〜ない

> Similar to: *to itte (mo) ii hodo*
>
> X *to itte (mo) ii kurai*
> Although one cannot state that something is X, it is nearly
> equivalent to X.
>
> See also: **kurai**

ノーベル賞作家が来週やって来るが、彼女の話は、授業を休んで
まで聞きに行く（という）ほどのことはない。

The author who won the Nobel Prize will come next week, but her talk is
not (important) enough for you to skip classes.

彼の今度の劇は非常に面白いが、ブロードウエーに出してもいい
（という）ほどの劇ではない。

His recent play is very interesting, but it is not so good that it could make
it to Broadway.

to iu imi de　という意味で　See　imi de

to iu ka　というか

> X *to iu ka*
> Raises doubts as to whether X is the appropriate word to use.

昨日のテストは難しかったというか、授業で習わなかったことば
かり出て全然出来なかった。

I don't know if "difficult" is the right word for the test we had yesterday,
but it was made up entirely of things we hadn't learned in class, and I
couldn't do it at all.

親友だと思っていた中山さんが私のことを悪く言っているときい
て、びっくりする<u>というか</u>、悲しくなってしまった。

Hearing that Nakayama, who I thought was a good friend, had been
saying bad things about me, I was surprised—if that is the right word—
and felt sad.

to iu koto　というこ と

> Similar to: *sō da*; *to no koto da*
>
> X *to iu koto*
> I hear X; I am told X, where X is secondhand information.

国体の開会式にこの県の知事が出席する<u>というこ と</u>だ。

I'm told that the prefectural governor will attend the opening ceremony
of the national athletic meet.

来年はまた授業料が上がる<u>というこ と</u>だ。

I hear that tuition will go up again next year.

to iu koto ni naru to　ということになると

> when it comes to
> Similar to: *to iu koto ni kakete wa*
>
> N *to iu koto ni naru to*
> When it comes to N.
>
> See also: **to kitara; to kuru to; to naru to**

子供の教育<u>ということになると</u>山口さんは金を惜しまない。

When it comes to his/her children's education, Yamaguchi doesn't care how much it costs.

車の修理<u>ということになると</u>カーターさんをおいて他にない。

When it comes to repairing cars, there is no one better than Carter.

to iu no wa　というのは

(1)
> X *to iu no wa*
> The thing called X; that which we call X.
>
> See also: **to iu no wa . . . (no) koto o iu**

"Sexual harassment" <u>というのは</u>、日本語でセクハラという。

"Sexual harassment" in Japanese is "*sekuhara*."

豆腐<u>というのは</u>、代表的な大豆食品である。

Tofu is a representative soybean product.

(2)
> X *to iu no wa*
> X. *To iu no wa*
> The reason for X. Can be used, as in the third and fourth examples below, as the continuation or elaboration of information contained in a previous sentence or passage, in the sense of "That is to say," "What I mean to say is . . ." or "The reason is . . ."
> Often paired with *kara* when giving explanations or reasons.

大都会に住みたくない<u>というのは</u>、大気汚染で頭が痛くなるから
である。

The reason I don't want to live in a big city is that the air pollution gives
me a headache.

私にとってはスペイン語より日本語を勉強する方がずっと面白い
<u>というのは</u>、日本語は私の母語である英語とあまりにも違ってい
るからである。

The reason I prefer studying Japanese to Spanish is that Japanese is so
different from English, my native tongue.

今年、ヨーロッパに行かないことにした。<u>というのは</u>、もう少し
お金をためてから行きたいからである。

I decided not to go to Europe this year. The reason is that I want to go
after I save a little more money.

今晩映画を見に行く約束をしていたが行けなくなった。<u>というの</u>
<u>は</u>、両親が急にやって来ることになったからである。

Although I promised to go to the movies tonight, I can't. The reason is
that at the last moment it turned out that my parents are coming over.

to iu no wa . . . (no) koto o iu   というのは～（の）ことを言う

> X *to iu no wa* Y *(no) koto o iu*, where *no* is used when Y is a noun.
> X is defined by Y.
>
> See also: **to iu no wa (1)**

198

歴史小説<u>というのは</u>歴史上の事件を題材にした小説<u>のことを言う</u>。

What we call the historical novel refers to a novel that takes historical events as its subject matter.

ブランチ<u>というのは</u>朝食と昼食を一緒にした食事<u>のことを言う</u>。

"Brunch" refers to breakfast and lunch combined.

to iu ten de wa　という点では

> With respect to; in that
> Similar to: *to iu koto ni kanshite wa*
>
> X *to iu ten de wa* Y
> With respect to X, Y is the case. Other aspects of a matter are unknown but at least as far as X is concerned, we can say Y.

日本は学歴社会である<u>という点では</u>、他のアジアの国々とあまり変わりがない。

Japan is not all that different from other Asian countries in that its society is based on academic qualifications.

いつも忙しくて暇がない<u>という点では</u>、田中さんも山田さんも同じである。

With respect to their being always busy and never having free time, Tanaka and Yamada are identical.

政治に関する知識<u>という点では</u>、カーターよりクリントンの方が上だといえる。

With respect to knowledge about politics, one can say that Clinton is superior to Carter.

<ruby>芸術的効果<rt>げいじゅつてきこうか</rt></ruby>という点では、カラーより<ruby>白黒<rt>しろくろ</rt></ruby>の<ruby>映画<rt>えいが</rt></ruby>の<ruby>方<rt>ほう</rt></ruby>がいいこと
もある。

In terms of artistic effects, black and white films are in some respects
superior to color.

to iu wake de wa nai　というわけではない　See **wake de wa nai**

to iu wake ni wa ikanai　というわけにはいかない　See **wake ni wa ikanai**

to iu yō na koto というようなこと

---

things like

X *to iu yō na koto*, where X can be a phrase or a sentence.
Things like X.

See also: **to itta yō na mono**; **yō na**

あの<ruby>魚嫌<rt>さかなぎら</rt></ruby>いの<ruby>渡辺<rt>わたなべ</rt></ruby>さんが、いかのさしみを食べるというようなこ
とはないと思う。

Watanabe, who hates seafood, probably wouldn't do something like eat
raw squid.

<ruby>今<rt>いま</rt></ruby><ruby>経済<rt>けいざい</rt></ruby>が<ruby>安定<rt>あんてい</rt></ruby>していないから、ドルの<ruby>価値<rt>かち</rt></ruby>が<ruby>急激<rt>きゅうげき</rt></ruby>に<ruby>変化<rt>へんか</rt></ruby>するとい
うようなことがあるかもしれない。

Because the economy now is unstable, something like a dramatic
fluctuation in the value of the dollar could occur.

to iu yō na mono　というようなもの　See **to itta yō na mono**

to iu yori hoka ni michi wa nai　というよりほかに途はない　See **(yori) hoka (ni) michi ga nai**

to iwarete iru　と言われている

> It is said that . . .
>
> X *to iwarete iru*
> X is said; it is said that something is X.

キムさんはこの<ruby>学校<rt>がっこう</rt></ruby>で<ruby>一番<rt>いちばん</rt></ruby>よく<ruby>出来<rt>でき</rt></ruby>る学生だ<u>と言われている</u>。

It is said that Kim is the best student in this school.

この大学には<ruby>山本<rt>やまもと</rt></ruby>さんくらい<ruby>上手<rt>じょうず</rt></ruby>にピアノがひきこなせる人はいないだろう<u>と言われている</u>。

It is said that in this university there is not likely to be anyone who can play the piano as well as Yamamoto.

to iwazu . . . to iwazu　と言わず〜と言わず

> whether . . . or . . .
> Similar to: *demo . . . demo*
>
> X *to iwazu* Y *to iwazu*, where both X and Y are nouns.
> Whether X or Y. X and Y are given as examples in what could be a much longer list.
> Often X and Y are pairs, such as adult and child, male and female, and so forth.
>
> See also: **ni shiro . . . ni shiro**

碁
ご
は大人
おとな
と言わず子供
こども
と言わず、誰
だれ
でも楽
たの
しめるものである。

The game of go is fun for everyone, whether adult or child.

金持
かねも
ちと言わず貧乏人
びんぼうにん
と言わず、誰
だれ
でも投票
とうひょう
する権利
けんり
がある。

Everyone, whether rich or poor, has the right to vote.

toka　とか

> Similar to: *to yara*
>
> X *toka*
> X or something／someone.
> Used when one is not entirely sure of X.
>
> See also: **yara**

山口
やまぐち
さんとかいう学生がこのレポートを西山教授
にしやまきょうじゅ
に渡
わた
して欲
ほ
しい

とおいていった。

A student whose name was Yamaguchi or something left this report, saying that s/he wanted it given to Professor Nishiyama.

松本さんが柔道部をやめる<u>とか</u>聞いたが、本当だろうか。

I heard something about Matsumoto quitting the judo club. Could it be true?

to kitara　ときたら

> when it comes to; as for
>
> N *to kitara* X
> When it comes to N, X.
> *To kitara* functions similarly to *to kuru to*, but it has an additional usage: N *to kitara* X is used when expressing something unfavorable such as a complaint or a criticism, either about the speaker him/herself or about someone else.
>
> See also: **to kuru to; to naru to**

大江さんのお兄さん<u>ときたら</u>、うるさくていつも妹さんの心配ばかりしている。

As for Ōe's older brother, he is very fussy and is always worrying about his younger sister.

今度の領事<u>ときたら</u>、英語もろくに話せない。

When it comes to the new consul, s/he can't even speak English very well.

tokoro de　ところで

---

even if; no matter

V-*ta tokoro de* X
Even if V takes place, the result will be a none-too-favorable X.
Often used with constructions such as *donna ni* . . . V-*ta tokoro de*
and *tatoe* . . .V-*ta tokoro de.*

See also:　**ni shiro; ni shite mo (2); tatoe . . . -te mo**

どんなに頑張ってみた<u>ところで</u>、締切りまであと二日しかないの
だから、どうにもなるまい。

No matter how hard I work, only two days are left until the deadline, so
there is nothing I can do about it now.

青島さんはもともとあまり賢くないので、大学に行った<u>ところ</u>
<u>で</u>、別に役に立つというわけでもないと思うが。

Aoshima is not very bright, so even if s/he goes to college, I don't think it
will do her/him any particular good.

tokoro (ga)　ところ（が）

---

although; even though

V-*ta tokoro (ga)* X
When V was done, X—something contrary to one's
expectations—happened.

せっかく時間をかけてパーティーの準備をした<u>ところが</u>、誰も来
てくれなかった。

Although I spent time preparing for the party, nobody came.

<ruby>徹夜<rt>てつや</rt></ruby>で<ruby>準備<rt>じゅんび</rt></ruby>して<ruby>授業<rt>じゅぎょう</rt></ruby>に<ruby>出<rt>で</rt></ruby>た<u>ところ</u>、<ruby>試験<rt>しけん</rt></ruby>は<ruby>来週<rt>らいしゅう</rt></ruby>になった。

I studied all night before going to class, and then the test was put off until next week!

to kurabete　と比べて　See **ni kurabete**

to kuru to　とくると

> as for; when it comes to
>
> N *to kuru to* X
> When it comes to N, X.
> Sets off N as the focus or topic of further comment.
>
> See also: **to iu koto ni naru to**; **to kitara**; **to naru to**

<ruby>母<rt>はは</rt></ruby>の<ruby>日<rt>ひ</rt></ruby>の<ruby>花<rt>はな</rt></ruby><u>とくると</u>、<ruby>日本<rt></rt></ruby>ではやはりカーネーションである。

When it comes to flowers for Mother's Day, carnations are given in Japan.

<ruby>中華料理<rt>ちゅうかりょうり</rt></ruby>の<ruby>中<rt>なか</rt></ruby>で<ruby>一番<rt>いちばん</rt></ruby>おいしいもの<u>とくると</u>、どうしても<ruby>鴨<rt>かも</rt></ruby><ruby>料理<rt></rt></ruby>と言わざるをえない。

When it comes to the most delicious of Chinese foods, one has to say that it is duck.

to mireba　とみれば　See **ka to miru to**

to miru to　とみると　See **ka to miru to**

205

to (mo) arō　と(も)あろう

> N *to (mo) arō* X
> X who is expected to be N.
> N represents someone or something worthy of high expectations.
> X is usually *mono* or *hito*. The writer conveys his/her displeasure
> that a person (X) who is supposed to be N has fallen short. Often
> used with *nanigoto da* to express "What is the world coming to
> when . . . !"
>
> See also: **to wa nanigoto da**

大学教授と(も)あろうものが人殺しをするとは何事だ。

What are we coming to when someone who is a university professor
commits a murder!

日本語の五年生と(も)あろうものがこんなやさしい文が読めない
とは何事だ。

What's going on when fifth-year students can't read sentences as easy as
these?

to (mo) naku　と(も)なく

> X *to (mo) naku*, where X is an interrogative.
> *To (mo) naku* adds uncertainty, as in *itsu kara to (mo) naku* (I don't
> know when).

野球の試合の後で、バーへ行って飲もうと誰からと(も)なく言い
出してみんなで出かけた。

After the baseball game, someone or other started talking about going to
a bar for a drink, so all of us went.

スーパーマンはどこから<u>と(も)なく</u>やって来て人助_{ひとだす}けをする。

Superman will come from somewhere and save people.

春_{はる}うららかな午後_{ごご}、小鳥_{ことり}が一羽_{いちわ}、どこから<u>と(も)なく</u>飛_とんでき
て、どこへ<u>と(も)なく</u>飛んで行った。

On a nice spring afternoon, a small bird flew up to me from somewhere
and then flew off again.

to mo natte iru   ともなっている

> N *to mo natte iru*
> Become N, among other things. Thus, the topic is not limited to N
> and is more encompassing than N.

この店_{みせ}のおかしはこの町_{まち}の名物_{めいぶつ}<u>ともなっている</u>。

This store's sweets have become one of this town's famous products.

あの先生の講義_{こうぎ}は非常_{ひじょう}に面白_{おもしろ}くて、この大学のよびもの<u>ともなっ
ている</u>。

Being extremely interesting, that professor's lectures have become one of
the attractions of this university.

tomo ni   共に   See to tomo ni

to nareba   となれば   See to naru to

to naru to　となると

> as for; when it comes to
> Similar to: *to natte wa; to nareba*
>
> N *to naru to*
> When it comes to N.
> This pattern differs from the simple topic marker *wa* in that it does more than single out a topic. It suggests something like "I am not interested in other matters, but when it comes to X . . . " *To naru to* may be replaced by either *to natte wa* or *to nareba*.
>
> See also: **to iu koto ni naru to; to kitara; to kuru to**

指導教官のブラウン教授の意見となると、無視するわけにはいかないだろう。

When it comes to my adviser Professor Brown's opinion, I can't very well ignore it.

あの先生のクイズはとてもやさしいので、全然勉強しなくても百点がとれるが、期末試験となると少し勉強しておいた方がいいかもしれない。

That professor's quizzes are very easy, so you can get a perfect score on them even if you don't study at all. But when it comes to the final, it's probably a good idea to study a little.

to natte wa　となっては　See **to naru to**

to no koto da　とのことだ

> I hear that; I am told that
> Similar to: *sō da*
>
> X *to no koto da*
> I hear X; I am told X, where X is secondhand information or hearsay.

今年の冬は例年になく寒くなる<u>とのことである</u>。

The report is that it will become unusually cold this winter.

村上さんは去年の十二月以来病気だ<u>とのことだ</u>。

I am told that Murakami has been ill since last December.

to onajiku　と同じく

> in the same way
> Similar to: *to dōyō ni; to onaji yō ni*
>
> N *to onajiku*
> In the same way as N; similar to N.
> A classical adverbial form of *onaji*.

日本語の二年生のクラスでも一年生の時<u>と同じく</u>ほとんど毎日クイズがある。

In the second-year Japanese class, too, there are quizzes almost every day, just as in the first year.

今日も昨日<u>と同じく</u>晴天である。

Today is a clear day, too—just the same as yesterday.

209

tōri　とおり［通り］

> as; in the same way as
> Similar to: *to onaji yō ni*
>
> X *tōri*
> As X; in the same way as X.
> When X is a noun, the pronunciation is *dōri* unless *no* follows the
> noun. When X is a word such as *sono* or *kono*, the expression is
> *sono tōri* or *kono tōri*.

この仕事は言われたとおりにやる限り、全然問題がないはずである。

As long as you do this work the way you were told, I expect there will be
no problems at all.

約束どおり、どんなことがあってもこの仕事は来週までに終わる
つもりだ。

As promised, I plan to finish the work by next week no matter what.

あなたの計画のとおりに全てうまくいくはずだ。

I expect everything to go successfully according to your plan.

tori mo naosazu　とりもなおさず

> namely; that is to say; in other words
> Similar to: *sunawachi*
>
> X *tori mo naosazu* Y
> X. *Tori mo naosazu* Y.
> X, that is to say, Y. X is explained in other words in Y.

ジョーンズさんは何でもよく知っている。<u>とりもなおさず</u>、生き字引である。

Jones knows everything—in other words, s/he is a living dictionary.

学費を払ってくれていた父がなくなった。父の死は<u>とりもなおさず</u>自活しなければならないことを意味する。

My father, who was paying my tuition, died. My father's death, in other words, means that I have to support myself.

to shitara としたら See **to suru to**

tōshite 通して See **tsūjite**

to shite mo としても See **ni shite mo (1)**

to sureba とすれば See **to suru to**

to suru とする See **ni suru**

to suru to　とすると

> assuming that; if we assume that
> Similar to: *to shitara; to sureba*
>
> X *to suru to* Y
> Assuming that X is the case, Y; if X is the case, then Y.
> *To suru to* may be replaced by *to sureba* or *to shitara*.

この件に関しては、山本さんと私だけしか知らないはずである
が、もし西田さんが知っているとすると、大変である。

I expect that only Yamamoto and I know about this matter. But if we
assume that Nishida knows, it's a problem.

彼のいうことが真実だとしたら、非常にめでたいことである。

If we could assume that what he says is true, it would be a wonderful
thing.

totan (ni)　とたん(に)〔途端(に)〕

> immediately after; as soon as
> Similar to: *suru to sugu ni; to hotondo dōji ni*
>
> V-*ta totan (ni)* X
> Immediately after V, X occurs.
> Although the verb is in the *-ta* form, X can be past, present, or
> future.
>
> See also: **ga hayai ka; ka to miru to; nari (1); ya ina ya**

今度の選挙で私は民主党を支持すると言ったとたんに、父は嫌な
顔をした。

As soon as I said that I would support the Democratic party in the
upcoming election, my father made a face.

212

じゅぎょう お　　　　　　こども　　　と　　　　いえ　かえ
授業が終わった<u>とたんに</u>、子供たちは飛ぶように家に帰ってしまう。

As soon as classes are over, the children will race home.

to tomo ni　と共に

> with; together with
> Similar to: *to issho ni*
>
> X *to tomo ni* Y
> Y along with X; Y together with X.

かぜ　　　　　さ
『風<u>と共に</u>去りぬ』は日本でもよく読まれている。

Gone with the Wind is widely read in Japan, too.

けいざいてき　はってん　　　　　　　こくさいしゃかい　　　じゅうよう　ち い
日本は経済的に発展する<u>と共に</u>、国際社会において重要な地位を
し
占めるようになった。

As Japan has developed economically, it has come to occupy an
important place in the international community.

totte　とって　See **ni totte**

to wa　とは

> X *to wa*
> Used in defining X or setting it off as the topic of discussion.
>
> See also: **to iu no wa (1)**; **to iu no wa . . . (no) koto o iu**

ブランチ<u>とは</u>朝食と昼食を一緒にしたものである。

"Brunch" is breakfast and lunch combined.

肥後<u>とは</u>現在の熊本のことである。

"Higo" refers to present-day Kumamoto.

to wa ie　**とは言え**

> however; although; but
> Similar to: *to itte mo; to iu keredomo*
>
> X *to wa ie* Y
> X is true, but what follows in Y may be contradictory.

岡田さんはいくらいい人だ<u>とは言え</u>、全財産を大学に寄付してしまうほどお人好しではない。

No matter how nice a person Okada may be, s/he is nonetheless not so naive as to donate his/her entire fortune to the university.

あの大学は大きな州立大学である<u>とは言え</u>、一人一人の学生を大切にする。

Although that university is a big state university, it values each individual student.

東京の冬はそれほど寒くない<u>とは言え</u>、セーターなしでは生活出来ない。

Although Tokyo winters are not that cold, you can't get along without a sweater.

to (wa) iwanu made mo　と（は）言わぬまでも

> V *to (wa) iwanu made mo* X, where V is negative.
> The suggestion is that one need not go as far as V for X to be the case.

彼女は天才だ<u>と（は）言わぬまでも</u>、非常に頭がいいと言える。

Without going so far as to say she is a genius, I must admit that she is nevertheless very smart.

あのホテルは一流<u>と（は）言わぬまでも</u>、たしかに立派な設備が整っている。

While I'm not saying that hotel is first class, it certainly is well-equipped.

to (wa) kagiranai　と（は）限らない

> not necessarily the case
> Similar to: *to (wa) kimatte inai*
>
> X *to (wa) kagiranai*
> X is not necessarily the case, despite general expectations. Suggests that there is more to a matter than merely X. Very frequently occurs with *kanarazu shimo*.

頭がいいからといって、成功する<u>と（は）限らない</u>。

Because one is smart does not necessarily mean that one will be successful.

体の大きい人が必ずしも力がある<u>と（は）限らない</u>。

Large people are not necessarily strong.

215

吉田さんは非常に頭がいいが、いつも百点だと(は)限らない。

Yoshida is extremely bright, but it is not necessarily the case that s/he always gets perfect scores.

to wa nanigoto da　とは何事だ

> X *to wa nanigoto da*
> A strong emphatic statement that X is unacceptable.
>
> See also: **to (mo) arō**

面接に遅れて来るとは何事だ。

How dare you come to an interview late?

警官でありながら、盗みをはたらくとは何事だ。

What have we come to when even police officers commit robberies!

towazu　問わず

> without regard to; regardless of
> Similar to: *ni kankei naku ichiō ni*; *o mondai ni sezu*
>
> N *o towazu*
> Without regard to N; regardless of N. N is often a *kanji* compound of complementary opposites such as *danjo* (men and women) and *naigai* (inside and outside; inner and outer).
>
> See also: **ni kakawarazu**

この仕事は男女の別を問わず、誰でも応募できる。

Anyone, regardless of gender, can apply for this job.

216

駅前のデパートは、週末、週日を問わず、賑わっている。

The department store in front of the station is busy regardless of whether it is a weekend or a weekday.

to yara　とやら　See **yara**

tsūjite　通じて

---

(1)　similar to: *ni watatte*

N *o tsūjite*
Throughout N, where N is a place or a time interval.

この地方は一年を通じて、雨が多い。

In this area there is a lot of rain all year long.

日本列島を通じて、台風の被害が見られた。

Damage from the typhoon was seen throughout the Japanese archipelago.

(2) | by means of; through
Similar to: *keiyu shite; shudan to shite; tōshite*

N *o tsūjite*
Through N; by means of N, where N acts as an agent.
Tōshite and *tsūjite* are often interchangeable. For example, both *tōshite* and *tsūjite* can be used in the sentences below without a change in nuance. *Tōshite* and *tsūjite* do not directly pinpoint the original source of information: regardless of the original source, the information comes through N. *Ni yotte*, in contrast, clearly indicates the source.
Naomi *ni yotte*, in the third sentence below, would indicate that Naomi is the original source.

See also: **ni yotte**

阪神大震災のニュースは衛星放送を通じて全世界に報道された。

News of the Great Kobe Earthquake was reported by satellite throughout the world.

三浦さんとは仕事を通じて知り合った。

I became acquainted with Miura through work.

林明氏の結婚を妹の直美を通じて知らされた。

I was informed of Mr. Hayashi Akira's marriage by my younger sister, Naomi.

tsuke . . . tsuke つけ〜つけ See **ni tsuke . . . ni tsuke**

tsukete つけて See **ni tsuke(te)**

tsuki つき See ni tsuki

tsumori つもり

> V-*ta tsumori*
> I thought I had V-ed, but . . .
> Beginning students of Japanese learn that *tsumori* indicates a
> writer's intention. However, when V is in the *-ta* form, *tsumori*
> indicates something the writer believes to be the case even when it
> is not.

消<ruby>け</ruby>したつもりの火<ruby>ひ</ruby>が燃<ruby>も</ruby>え上<ruby>あ</ruby>がって火事<ruby>かじ</ruby>になってしまった。

The fire I thought I had doused burst into flames and ended up a blaze.

たばこはやめたつもりだったが、ストレスがたまって我慢<ruby>がまん</ruby>しきれ
なくなり、また吸<ruby>す</ruby>い出<ruby>だ</ruby>した。

I was sure I was through with smoking, but stress built up and I was
unable to stand it, so I started smoking again.

tsure(te) つれ（て） See ni tsure(te)

-tsutsu -つつ

> at the same time; while
> Similar to: *nagara*
>
> V-stem-*tsutsu* X
> X occurs at the same time as V; X is simultaneous with V.

219

子供を育て<u>つつ</u>仕事をするのは大変なことである。

To work while raising a child is a very difficult thing.

スポーツをやり<u>つつ</u>いい成績を保つのは難しい。

It is difficult to maintain good grades while participating in sports.

-tsutsu aru   -つつある

---

in the process of
Similar to: *kakatte iru*

V-stem-*tsutsu aru*
In the process of V-ing.

この国の経済は発展し<u>つつある</u>。

The economy of this country is in the process of developing.

米国においては昔ながらの伝統的な美徳が失われ<u>つつある</u>と言われている。

It is said that in the United States old-fashioned traditional virtues are in the process of being lost.

U

uchi ni　うちに　See **nai uchi ni**

ue de　上で

(1)
> in terms of; in the field of; in order to; for the purpose of
> Similar to: *ten de*
>
> X *(no) ue (de)*, where *no* is used when X is a noun.
> About X; in terms of X; in the field of X.
>
> See also: **jō (1)**

個人間の約束を破るということは、法律の<u>上</u>(で)問題にならない
かもしれないが、道義上問題になる。

In terms of the law, breaking a promise between individuals may not be a
problem; but from the perspective of ethics, it is problematic.

学問の<u>上</u>(で)の議論はすればするほど役に立つものである。

The more debate there is in academics, the more useful it is.

外国語を学習する<u>上</u>(で)大切なことは毎日の努力がものを言うと
いうことである。

In studying a foreign language, what is important is the everyday effort.

人と上手に付き合う上(で)誠実であることが第一条件と言えるかもしれない。

In getting along well with others, it is perhaps fair to say that sincerity is the most important aspect.

---

(2) after
Similar to: *ato de*

X *(no) ue (de)*, where *no* is used when X is a noun. When X is a verb, the *-ta* form is used.
After X; after X takes place.

その家を買うかどうかは、よく調べた上(で)決めるつもりである。

I plan to decide on whether or not to buy that house after thorough investigation.

その件については家族と相談の上(で)返事をするようにする。

I will respond concerning that matter after talking it over with my family.

---

ue (ni)　上(に)

---

on top of; in addition to; beyond
Similar to: *dake de naku; no ni kuwaete*

X *(no) ue (ni)*, where *no* is used when X is a noun.
On top of X; in addition to X.

See also: **bakari ka**

日本は耕地が狭い上(に)、天然資源が少ない。

In addition to having limited arable land, Japan has few natural resources.

カレーライスは用意するのが簡単な<u>上（に）</u>、安く済むので学生が好んで作るようである。

It seems that students enjoy making curried rice because, on top of being easy to prepare, it can be made cheaply.

彼は一日中工場で重労働の<u>上（に）</u>、家に帰っても病気の両親の世話で休むことも出来ない。

In addition to working hard all day long in a factory, he can't rest even after returning home, because he has to look after his sick parents.

ue wa　上は

> as long as; so long as
>
> X *ue wa* Y
> As long as X has happened, Y; as long as one is involved in X, Y.
>
> See also: **ijō (wa)**; **kagiri (1)**

みんなの意見がこうバラバラでまとまりがない<u>上は</u>、投票によって決定せざるをえないことになるだろう。

As long as everyone's opinions diverge like this, I think it will probably become necessary to decide by vote.

語学を必修課目からはずすという考えには賛成ではないが、教授会で決定された<u>上は</u>、従うよりほか仕方がない。

I don't agree with the idea of removing language study from required coursework, but as long as it has been decided at a faculty meeting, there is nothing to do but go along with the decision.

-uru   -得る

> able to; can do
> Similar to: *koto ga dekiru*
>
> V-stem-*uru*
> Able to V.
> The *-ta* form of *-uru* is read *-eta* not *-uta*.
>
> See also: **arienai; -enai; -zaru o enai**

これは非常に難しい問題だ。この問題を解き<u>得る</u>のは彼以外には
いない。

This is a very difficult problem. No one can solve it but him.

コンコルドでもニューヨークからパリまでそんなに短時間で行き
<u>得る</u>はずがない。

You can't expect to go from New York to Paris in such a short time even
by (flying) the Concorde.

ピアニストの彼にとって、カーネギーホールで演奏し<u>得た</u>ことが
彼の生涯の中で最も喜ばしいことであった。

For a pianist like him, being able to perform at Carnegie Hall was the
most thrilling experience of his life.

W

wake da   わけだ［訳だ］

> X *wake da*
> That's why X; that's the reason why X; it is the case that X.
> X is a matter of course, something that naturally follows from what is said earlier or something that one is led to understand.
>
> See also: **imi suru**; **koto ni naru (2)**

<ruby>外交官<rt>がいこうかん</rt></ruby>になりたいから<ruby>国際政治<rt>こくさいせいじ</rt></ruby>を<ruby>専攻<rt>せんこう</rt></ruby>している<u>わけである</u>。

I want to become a diplomat, and so that is why I am majoring in international politics.

<ruby>日本<rt></rt></ruby>は<ruby>土地<rt>とち</rt></ruby>が<ruby>狭<rt>せま</rt></ruby>く、人が<ruby>多<rt>おお</rt></ruby>いので<ruby>人口密度<rt>じんこうみつど</rt></ruby>が<ruby>高<rt>たか</rt></ruby>い<u>わけだ</u>。

Japan has little land and many people, and so that is why the population density is high.

wake de wa nai   わけではない［訳ではない］

> Similar to: *toku ni sono yō na koto wa nai*
>
> X *wake de wa nai*
> It does not follow that X is the case; something is not particularly X; the assumption that X is the case is unwarranted.

日本文学を教えているからといって日本文学が専門だというわけではない。ただちょっと文学をかじったという程度であるに過ぎない。

Even though I am teaching Japanese literature, it doesn't necessarily follow that my specialty is Japanese literature. It only means that I know a bit about literature.

兄は四十才で独身であるが、結婚したくないわけではない。適当な人がいないだけである。

My brother is forty and single, but that doesn't mean he doesn't want to get married. It's just that there's no suitable person.

wake ni wa ikanai　わけにはいかない［訳にはいかない］

it won't do; one can't very well

X *wake ni wa ikanai*
X won't do; X is not at all the case.
While X is a theoretical possibility, there are strong reasons why in practice X is not at all the case, not possible.
Contrast with *wake de wa nai*, where that which is negated is a matter of course, following from the information given. Here the meaning is closer to "should not," rather than "is not." The negation derives from strong moral or psychological imperatives rather than from something that is natural or a matter of course.

アメリカはいくら自由な国だからといって、子供を学校に行かせないわけにはいかない。

No matter how free a country the United States is, one can't very well not send one's children to school.

226

<ruby>残業<rt>ざんぎょう</rt></ruby>しないで<ruby>帰<rt>かえ</rt></ruby>りたいのだが、まだ<ruby>部長<rt>ぶちょう</rt></ruby>がのこっているので帰る<u>わけにはいかない</u>。

I'd like to go home without staying late at work, but my section head is still here, so I can't very well go home.

wa shimai　はしまい

> surely not; definitely not
>
> V-stem *wa shimai*
> V will not be the case.
> A stronger and more emphatic negative form than a simple V-*mai* form. In the case of the verb *suru*, *suru mai*, *shimai*, and *sumai* can all be used without changing the meaning.
>
> See also: **-mai ka**

<ruby>藤田<rt>ふじた</rt></ruby>さんは<ruby>周<rt>まわ</rt></ruby>りの<ruby>人々<rt>ひとびと</rt></ruby>から<ruby>尊敬<rt>そんけい</rt></ruby>されている<ruby>立派<rt>りっぱ</rt></ruby>な人である。いくら<ruby>山本<rt>やまもと</rt></ruby>さんのことが気に入らないからと<ruby>言<rt>い</rt></ruby>って、山本さんの<ruby>悪口<rt>わるくち</rt></ruby>など言い<u>はしまい</u>。

Fujita is a great person who is respected by those around him/her. No matter how much s/he cannot stomach Yamamoto, s/he will surely not speak ill of her/him.

ウォーカーさんはベジタリアンだということだから、このハムサンドイッチも食べ<u>はしまい</u>。

I understand that Walker is a vegetarian, so s/he will certainly not eat this ham sandwich.

wa shinai　はしない

> absolutely not; definitely not
> V-stem *wa shinai*
>
> A strong, emphatic negation of V. This pattern is often used in describing unfavorable situations and conveys the speaker's strong emotions.
>
> See also: **ari wa shinai**; **mo shinai**; **-te i wa shinai**

長谷川さんはいつも遊びに来ると言っているが、いくら招いても
一度も来<u>はしない</u>。

Hasegawa is always saying that s/he will come see us, but no matter how often we extend an invitation, s/he has never come even once.

清水さんは新聞を四つもとっているが、一つも読み<u>はしない</u>。

Shimizu subscribes to four newspapers, but s/he doesn't even read one of them.

wa su(ru) mai　はす（る）まい　See **wa shimai**

Y

ya ina ya　やいなや[や否や]

> as soon as
> Similar to: *suru to sugu ni*
>
> V *ya ina ya* X, where V is in the citation form.
> As soon as V then X, where X occurs immediately after V.
>
> See also: **ga hayai ka; ka to miru to; nari (1); soba kara; totan (ni)**

あの会社の従業員は仕事を終える<u>やいなや</u>、バーにむかうようだ。

It seems that the employees of that company head for a bar as soon as they finish work.

私は大学を卒業する<u>やいなや</u>、親の家を出た。

As soon as I graduated from college, I moved out of my parents' house.

yamanai　やまない　See -te yamanai

yamu o enai　やむを得ない

> unavoidable; there is nothing one can do
> Similar to: *hoka ni hōhō ga nai; shikata ga nai*
>
> X *wa yamu o enai*
> *Yamu o enai* X
> X cannot be stopped; X is an inevitability; there is nothing one can
> do about X.
>
> See also: **yamu o ezu**

雪^{ゆき}のため、講師^{こうし}の乗^のった飛行機^{ひこうき}が遅^{おく}れ、講演^{こうえん}が中止^{ちゅうし}されたのは<u>や</u>
<u>むを得ない</u>。

On account of the snow the plane in which the speaker was riding was
late, and the canceling of the lecture was unavoidable.

<u>やむを得ない</u>事情^{じじょう}のため、大学を中退^{ちゅうたい}することになった。

Because of unavoidable circumstances, it was decided that I would leave
the university.

yamu o ezu　やむを得ず

> out of necessity; unavoidably
> Similar to: *shikata naku*
>
> *Yamu o ezu* X
> Although one does not wish to do X, there is no other choice, and
> so one does it out of necessity.
> Adverbial form of *yamu o enai*.
>
> See also: **yamu o enai**

今日は風邪をひいて気分が悪かったが、研究発表をすることに
なっていたので、<u>やむを得ず</u>、授業に出た。

Today I had a cold and was feeling bad, but since I was supposed to give
a research presentation in class, out of necessity I showed up in class.

同窓会の仕事など全然する気はなかったが、私が大学所在地に住
んでいるという関係上、<u>やむを得ず</u>、発起人にされてしまった。

I had absolutely no desire to work for the alumni association or anything
of the sort, but since I live in the university area, I inevitably ended up
being made the founder.

yara やら

> X *yara*
> Used in the same way as the question particle *ka* to indicate
> uncertainty. Often used in combination with question words.
>
> See also: **toka**

先日西田さんの家を訪問して彼のおばあさんにお目にかかった。
彼女は東北弁で何か私に話しかけてきたが、何のこと<u>やら</u>全然分
からなかった。

The other day I visited Nishida's home and met his grandmother. She
said something to me in Tōhoku dialect, but I had no idea what she was
saying.

久しぶりに友人と飲みに出かけ、話し込んでいるうちにいつの間
に<u>やら</u>十二時過ぎになってしまった。

I went out drinking with a friend I hadn't seen in a long time, and while
we were talking, before I knew it, it got to be past twelve o'clock.

むらさきしきぶ　いしやまでら　げんじものがたり　か　　　　　　　はなし　つた
紫式部は石山寺で源氏物語を書いたと<u>やら</u>いう話が伝わっている。

A story has been handed down saying something to the effect that
Murasaki Shikibu wrote *The Tale of Genji* at Ishiyama Temple.

なかやま　　　　　らいねん　　　　　　　たんしんふにん　　　　き
中山さんは来年、パリへ単身赴任すると<u>やら</u>聞いている。

I've heard something to the effect that next year Nakayama will be
working alone in Paris, away from his/her family.

yara . . . yara　やら〜やら

> and; and so forth
> Similar to: *ya*
>
> X *yara* Y *yara*, where X and Y are nouns.
> X, Y, and others. Suggests that there are more items than just X
> and Y in the list.
> Used in a manner similar to *ya* in enumerating things.

かいぎ　　　らいねん　よさん　ぎょうじ　　かん　はな　あ
今日の会議では来年の予算<u>やら</u>行事<u>やら</u>に関して話し合うことに
なっている。

At today's meeting we are supposed to discuss next year's budget and
events and things like that.

こんばん　　　　　　　　　　　たけうち　　　あおき
今晩のパーティーには、竹内さん<u>やら</u>青木さん<u>やら</u>くるというこ
とである。

It is the case that Takeuchi, Aoki, and others will come to the party
tonight.

-yō　-よう　See -ō

-yō de wa nai ka　-ようではないか　See **-ō de wa nai ka**

-yō ga . . . -mai ga　-ようが～-まいが　See **-ō ga . . . -mai ga**

-yō ga . . . -yō ga　-ようが～-ようが　See: **-ō ga . . . -ō ga**

-yō koto nara　-ようことなら　See **-ō koto nara**

-yō mono nara　-ようものなら　See **mono nara**

yō na　ような

---

like; similar to
Similar to: *nite iru*

X *(no) yō na* Y, where *no* is used when X is a noun.
Y that is similar to X; an X-like Y.

See also: **to itta yō na mono; to iu yō na koto**

一月だというのに、暖かくて春の<u>ような</u>天気だ。

Despite the fact that it is January, the weather is warm and springlike.

丸山さんの声はプレスリーの<u>ような</u>声だと言われている。

They say that Maruyama's voice is like Elvis Presley's.

233

<ruby>人<rt>ひと</rt></ruby>の<ruby>前<rt>まえ</rt></ruby>で<ruby>恥<rt>はじ</rt></ruby>をかく<u>ような</u>ことはしたくないものだ。

I do not want to do things that will embarrass me in front of other people.

yō ni　ように

> in order to; so that
>
> V *yō ni* X, where *no* is used when X is a noun.
> In order for V, X is done; for the purpose of V, X is done.

<ruby>早<rt>はや</rt></ruby>くテニスが<ruby>上手<rt>じょうず</rt></ruby>になる<u>ように</u><ruby>毎日練習<rt>まいにちれんしゅう</rt></ruby>している。

I'm practicing tennis every day in order to become good at it.

みんなに<ruby>見<rt>み</rt></ruby>える<u>ように</u><ruby>大<rt>おお</rt></ruby>きな<ruby>字<rt>じ</rt></ruby>で<ruby>書<rt>か</rt></ruby>いた。

I wrote in large letters so that they could be seen by everyone.

yō ni iu　ように言う

> tell someone to do something
>
> V *yō ni iu*
> Tell someone to do V.
> In place of *iu* other verbs like *chūi-suru* (warn someone), *oshieru* (teach someone), and *tanomu* (ask someone) may be used.

<ruby>今日<rt></rt></ruby>は<ruby>一日中<rt>いちにちじゅう</rt></ruby>、<ruby>家<rt>いえ</rt></ruby>にいないので、<ruby>十時過<rt>じゅうじす</rt></ruby>ぎに<ruby>電話<rt>でんわ</rt></ruby>する<u>ように言っ</u>

ておいた。

Because I won't be at home all day today, I told him/her (in advance) to

call me after ten.

<ruby>中<rt>なか</rt></ruby><ruby>野<rt>の</rt></ruby>さんはいつもたばこを<ruby>吸<rt>す</rt></ruby>っている。<ruby>少<rt>すく</rt></ruby>なくとも<ruby>教室<rt>きょうしつ</rt></ruby>では吸わ
ない<u>ように</u><ruby>注意<rt>ちゅうい</rt></ruby><u>した</u><ruby>方<rt>ほう</rt></ruby>がいい。

Nakano smokes all the time. We ought to warn him/her to not smoke in
the classroom at least.

yō ni naru　ようになる

> reach the point where . . .
>
> V *yō ni naru*
> Reach the point where V is possible. V is often a verb in the
> potential form.
> In contrast to both *yō ni suru* and *koto ni suru*, in which the
> speaker's intention is at work, in both *koto ni naru* and *yō ni naru*,
> the situation (V) turns out to be the case regardless of
> the speaker's intention, as seen in the following two sentences:
>
> (a) うちの<ruby>七才<rt>ななさい</rt></ruby>の<ruby>息子<rt>むすこ</rt></ruby>は学校まで<ruby>一人<rt>ひとり</rt></ruby>で<ruby>歩<rt>ある</rt></ruby>いて行く<u>ことになった</u>。
> It has been decided that my seven-year-old son will walk to
> school alone.
>
> (b) うちの<ruby>七才<rt>さい</rt></ruby>の<ruby>息子<rt>むすこ</rt></ruby>は学校まで<ruby>一人<rt>ひとり</rt></ruby>で<ruby>歩<rt>ある</rt></ruby>いて行ける<u>ようになった</u>。
> It has reached the point where my seven-year-old son can
> walk to school alone.

<ruby>長<rt>なが</rt></ruby>い<ruby>間<rt>あいだ</rt></ruby>勉強してやっとスペイン<ruby>語<rt>ご</rt></ruby>が<ruby>自由<rt>じゆう</rt></ruby>に<ruby>話<rt>はな</rt></ruby>せる<u>ようになった</u>か
らとてもうれしい。

I am very happy because, after having studied Spanish for a long time, I
have finally gotten to the point where I can speak it fluently.

<ruby>円高<rt>えんだか</rt></ruby>ドル<ruby>安<rt>やす</rt></ruby>のおかげで、<ruby>多<rt>おお</rt></ruby>くの日本人が<ruby>世界中<rt>せかいじゅう</rt></ruby>いろいろな<ruby>所<rt>ところ</rt></ruby>へ<ruby>出<rt>で</rt></ruby>かけて行く<u>ようになった</u>。

Thanks to the high value of the yen and cheap dollars, things have reached the point where a number of Japanese travel to various places throughout the world.

yō ni natte iru　ようになっている

> V *yō ni natte iru*
> Something has been done or arranged so that V.
> V *koto ni natte iru* is used for something that has become a practice; similarly, V*yō ni natte iru* is used for something that has become a practice or a rule. In the former, the practice is emphasized, whereas in the latter, the process by which V became a practice is emphasized.

<ruby>車<rt>くるま</rt></ruby>の<ruby>窓<rt>まど</rt></ruby>は<ruby>外<rt>そと</rt></ruby>から<ruby>開<rt>あ</rt></ruby>けられない<u>ようになっている</u>。

The windows of cars are made so that they cannot be opened from outside.

この<ruby>店<rt>みせ</rt></ruby>では、いろいろなクレジットカードが<ruby>使<rt>つか</rt></ruby>える<u>ようになっている</u>。

In this shop, (it has been arranged such that) various credit cards can be used.

yō ni shite iru　ようにしている

---

trying to; making an effort to

V *yō ni shite iru*
Making an effort to do V.
Used for actions that are not habits where the writer is trying to make the action habitual.This contrasts with *koto ni shite iru*, which indicates actions that have already become habitual.

スペイン語が上手になるように、毎日一時間ずつテープをきく<u>よ</u><u>うにしている</u>。

In order to become good at Spanish, I am trying to listen to tapes every day for an hour.

健康によくないので、酒を飲み過ぎない<u>ようにしている</u>。

Because it is not good for the health, I am making efforts not to drink too much.

yō ni suru　ようにする

---

make an effort to; make sure to

V *yō ni suru*
In such a way as to V; make sure to V.
V *yō ni suru* and V *koto ni suru* are both used when expressing a decision that was made by the speaker. V *koto ni suru* emphasizes that the decision was made. In contrast, V *yō ni suru* emphasizes the process or effort to do or not do something. In the two sets of sentences below, the outcome may be the same, but there is a slight difference in nuance:

(a) 肥らないように甘いものは食べない<u>ことにした</u>。
I have decided not to eat sweet things so that I will not get fat. (The emphasis is on the speaker's decision. We don't know whether s/he actually doesn't eat sweet things—we only know that s/he made a decision not to.)

(b) 肥らないように甘いものは食べない<u>ようにした</u>。
I acted in such a way as to not eat sweet things so that I wouldn't get fat. (The speaker still might have wanted to eat sweet things, but s/he did not eat them. The process by which s/he avoided eating them is emphasized.)

(c) 毎週芝をかる<u>ことにした</u>。
I decided to mow the lawn every week. (The speaker made the decision, but s/he may not have followed up on it. The decision is what is important.)

(d) 毎週芝をかる<u>ようにした</u>。
I acted in such a way as to mow the lawn every week. (The speaker mowed the lawn every week. The action of mowing the lawn is emphasized.)

留守中、犬の散歩を忘れない<u>ようにして</u>ください。

Please try not to forget to take the dog for a walk while I'm away.

<ruby>言葉<rt>ことば</rt></ruby>の勉強をする<ruby>時<rt>とき</rt></ruby>は<ruby>毎日<rt>まいにち</rt></ruby>テープを<ruby>聞<rt>き</rt></ruby>く<u>ようにした</u>方<rt>ほう</rt>がいい。

When studying languages, one had better make sure to listen to tapes every day.

yorazu よらず See **ni yorazu**

yori より See **ni yotte**

(yori) hoka (ni) michi ga nai　（より）ほか（に）途がない

---

there is no other way
Similar to: *hoka ni hōhō ga nai*

V *(yori) hoka (ni) michi ga nai*, where V is in the citation form. Other than V there is no other way; V is the only way to achieve the speaker's wish. The possibilities are limited to V. V is often followed by *yori*.

See also: **(yori) hoka (ni) shikata ga nai**

<ruby>一日<rt>いちにち</rt></ruby>も<ruby>早<rt>はや</rt></ruby>く<ruby>韓国<rt>かんこく</rt></ruby>に行きたいが、ビザが<ruby>出<rt>で</rt></ruby>るまで<ruby>待<rt>ま</rt></ruby>つ<u>（より）ほか（に）途がない</u>。

I want to go to Korea as soon as possible, but I have no choice but to wait for a visa.

アメリカの<ruby>大統領<rt>だいとうりょう</rt></ruby>はほとんど<ruby>外国語<rt>がいこくご</rt></ruby>ができないので、<ruby>通訳<rt>つうやく</rt></ruby>に<ruby>頼<rt>たよ</rt></ruby>る<u>ほか（に）途がない</u>。

Since for the most part American presidents cannot speak foreign languages, there is no other way but for them to depend on interpreters.

(yori) hoka (ni) shikata ga nai　（より）ほか（に）仕方がない

> there is no other way
>
> V *(yori) hoka (ni) shikata ga nai*, where V is in the citation form.
> There is no other way but V.　V is often followed by *yori*.
>
> See also:　**(yori) hoka (ni) michi ga nai**

ここからシカゴまで行くのには、飛行機が一番いいが、航空会社
がストライキ中だから、車で行く（より）ほか（に）仕方がない。

It's best to go from here to Chicago by plane, but the airline is now on
strike, so we have no choice but to go by car.

この教室はクーラーがないが、ほかに教室がないから、この教室
を使う（より）ほか（に）仕方がない。

This classroom has no air conditioning, but there are no other classrooms
available, so there is no other option but to use this room.

(yori) hoka (wa) nai　（より）ほか（は）　ない

> Similar to:　*shika nai*
>
> V *(yori) hoka (wa) nai*, where V is in the citation form.
> V is the only way.　There is no other way but V.

両親は彼女との結婚には反対だが、私としては、結婚するのは両
親ではなく私なのだという（より）ほか（は）ない。

My parents are against my marrying her.　But all I can say is that they are
not the ones getting married—I am.

すうがく　　　　　　　　　　　　もんだい
数学の先生がこんなにやさしい問題ができないのはどうかしている
　　　　　　　でき
というが、出来ないものは出来ないという<u>(より)ほか(は)ない</u>。

My math teacher says there's something wrong with someone who can't
do such an easy problem. But there's nothing else for me to say except
that I can't do what I can't do.

ふと　　　　あま
太るので甘いものは食べないことにしているのだが、折角私のため
　つく　　　　たんじょうび
に作ってくれた誕生日のケーキなので、食べる<u>よりほか(は)ない</u>。

I make it a rule not to eat sweet things because I'll get fat, but since it's a
birthday cake made especially for me, I have no choice but to eat it.

yoru　よる See **ni yoru**

yoru to　よると See **ni yoru to**

yoshi　よし[由]

> Similar to: *to iu koto; to no koto*
>
> X *(no) yoshi*, where *no* is used when X is a noun.
> I am told X; I hear that X.
> Describes something one has heard. Often used in letter writing.
> In sentence-medial position *yoshi* alone is correct; in sentence-final
> position, the copula follows.

たかぎ　　　　みょうにちづ　　　　　　　　　がくちょう
高木先生は明日付けであの大学の学長になられる<u>由</u>である。

I hear that starting tomorrow Professor Takagi will become the president
of that university.

内田さんのご子息が首席で大学ご卒業の<u>由</u>、めでたいことである。

I am told that Uchida's son graduated as valedictorian of his college. It was an auspicious event.

yoso ni　よそに

> ignoring; without regard to
> Similar to: *kaerimizu ni; kankei naku; mushi shite*
>
> X *o yoso ni* Y
> Regardless of X, Y.

兄は両親の心配を<u>よそに</u>、大学をやめてしまった。

Ignoring my parents' concerns, my older brother ended up dropping out of college.

患者の不安を<u>よそに</u>、医者は新しい薬品を使ってみることにした。

Disregarding the patient's uneasiness, the doctor decided to try using a new drug.

-yō to　-ようと　See -ō to

-yō to . . . -mai to　-ようと〜-まいと　See -ō ga . . . -mai ga

-yō to shinai　-ようとしない　See -ō to shinai

-yō to suru   -ようとする See **-ō to suru**

-yō to ... -yō to   -ようと〜-ようと See **-ō ga ... -ō ga**

yotte   よって See **ni yotte**

yue (ni)   ゆえ（に）［故(に)]

---

because
Similar to: *kara*; *no de*

X *(ga) yue (ni)* Y
Because of X, Y; X cites reasons for Y. X may also end a sentence,
with the following sentence beginning *sono/sore yue*, meaning
"Because of X . . . "
A classical expression not used in spoken Japanese.

祖母は昔の教育を受けた日本人であった（が）<u>ゆえ（に）</u>、昭和天皇
の写真を目にする度に、お辞儀をした。

Because my grandmother was a Japanese who received her education
long ago, every time she saw a picture of the Shōwa emperor, she bowed.

日本は小さな島国である（が）<u>故（に）</u>、多くのものを外国から輸入
しなくてはいけない。

Because Japan is a small island country, it must import many things from
abroad.

このところ、日本は不景気である。それ<u>故(に)</u>失業者の数が増え
ている。

Recently the Japanese economy has been bad. Because of that, the
number of unemployed has been increasing.

Z

-zaru o enai -ざるを得ない

> can't help but . . . ; have no choice but to . . .
>
> V-*zaru o enai*
> V is the only way.
> Often means that the speaker must do something against his/her
> will.

非常に疲れているが社長のパーティーなので、<u>行かざるを得ない</u>
だろう。

I'm very tired, but since it's the company president's party, I suppose I
have no choice but to go.

折角私のために友達が作ってくれたケーキだから、いくらダイ
エット中でも<u>食べざるを得ない</u>。

Because it is a cake that my friend went to the trouble to make for me, no
matter how much I am dieting, I have no choice but to eat some.

みうら　　　　あたま　　　　　　　　　　じゅぎょう　　　やす　　らくだいてん
三浦さんは頭のいい学生なのだが、授業をよく休むので落第点を

つけ<u>ざるを得なかった</u>。

Miura is a bright student but s/he often skips classes, so I had no choice
but to give her/him a failing grade.

-zu (ni)　-ず（に）

> without; instead of
> Similar to: *nai de*
>
> V-*zu (ni)*
> Without V-ing; instead of V-ing.
>
> See also: **-zu shite**

なに
何も食べ<u>ず（に）</u>アスピリンをのむと、気分が悪くなる。

When you take aspirin without eating anything, you feel bad.

か
このところ、買いたいものも買わ<u>ず（に）</u>、お金をためて旅行する

ことにしている。

Recently, instead of buying things I want, I have been saving money and
traveling.

ひ　しごと　　　　　　　　うみ
こんなに天気のいい日には仕事をせ<u>ず（に）</u>、海か山にでも行きた

いものだ。

On a day as nice as this I want to go to the sea or the mountains instead
of working.

-zu shite   -ずして

> without; instead of
> Similar to: *nai de*
>
> V-*zu shite*
> Without V-ing.
> A classical form of *nai de* or *zu ni*.
>
> See also: **-zu (ni)**

弟はよく考え<u>ずして</u>行動する傾向があるので、いつも注意するのだが、その癖はなかなか直らない。

My younger brother has a tendency to act without thinking, so I often have to tell him to be careful, but that habit of his does not die easily.

当大学山岳部はヒマラヤ山中で遭難し、飲まず食わ<u>ずして</u>三日三晩を過ごした。

The mountaineering club at this university had an accident in the Himalayas and spent three days and nights without eating or drinking.

zutto   ずっと

(1) | Used to describe extremes, often in comparisons.

今年の学生の方が去年の学生より<u>ずっと</u>明るい。

The students this year are much more lively than the students last year.

私が台湾に行ったのは<u>ずっと</u>昔のことである。

It was a long time ago when I went to Taiwan.

(2) | from beginning to end

春休み中、ずっと家に帰っていた。

During the spring vacation, I was home for the whole time.

今年の初めから休まずにずっと仕事をしているので、少し休暇を

とるつもりだ。

I have been working continuously from the beginning of this year, so I plan to take a little break.

Appendix A

ki ga aru　気がある be interested in

<ruby>隣<rt>となり</rt></ruby>の<ruby>娘<rt>むすめ</rt></ruby>はうちの<ruby>息子<rt>むすこ</rt></ruby>に<u>気がある</u>のか、よく電話をかけて来る。

I wonder if the girl next door is interested in my son. She often calls him.

ki ga au　気が合う get along with

<ruby>互<rt>たが</rt></ruby>いに<ruby>考<rt>かんが</rt></ruby>えが<ruby>違<rt>ちが</rt></ruby>っていても<u>気が合う</u>ということもある。

Even if we think about things differently, there are times when we agree.

ki ga chigau　気が違う be mad; be crazy

<ruby>当時<rt>とうじ</rt></ruby>の<ruby>人々<rt>ひとびと</rt></ruby>は<ruby>人間<rt>にんげん</rt></ruby>の<ruby>飛行<rt>ひこう</rt></ruby>を<ruby>考<rt>かんが</rt></ruby>えたダビンチを<u>気が違った</u>のではなかろうかと思った。

People contemporary with da Vinci thought that he must be crazy (because) he thought about human flight.

ki ga chiisai 気が小さい be timid; be cowardly

あんな気が小さい人間がギャンブルなどに手を出すはずがない。

There is no reason to believe that such a timid person would get involved in something like gambling.

ki ga chiru 気が散る be distracted

隣のラジオがうるさくて勉強しようとしても気が散る。

The radio next door is noisy, and even if I try to study, I get distracted.

ki ga fureru 気が触れる become mad; become crazy

ハムレットの心を測り兼ねて、オフィーリアは気が触れてしまった。

Unable to fathom Hamlet's heart, Ophelia went mad.

ki ga hareru 気が晴れる be spirited; feel lighthearted; be cheerful

本当に悲しい時は、なぐさめを言ってもらっても気が晴れるものではない。

When you are truly sad, it won't cheer you up even when someone comforts you.

ki ga haru 気が張る be tense; be anxious; have one's mind focused

忙しい時は気が張っているので、疲れに気が付かない。

Because your mind is focused on something when you are busy, you are not aware of being tired.

ki ga hayai　気が早い　be impatient; be hasty; be unable to wait

あの<u>気の早い</u>カップルは、まだ子供（こども）もいないのに、子供の教育（きょういく）を
論（ろん）じ合（あ）っている。

That impatient (overeager) couple is discussing with one another the
education of their children even though they don't have any yet.

ki ga hayaru　気がはやる　be anxious

初陣（ういじん）となると、手柄（てがら）を立（た）てなければと<u>気がはやる</u>。

When it comes to one's first battle, one is anxious to perform great deeds.

ki ga hazumu　気がはずむ　be excited

久（ひさ）しぶりの休暇（きゅうか）を前（まえ）にして<u>気がはずむ</u>。

I'm excited in anticipation of my long-awaited vacation.

ki ga hikeru　気が引ける　be ashamed of; be self-conscious; be ill at ease

同僚（どうりょう）を我（わ）が家（や）に招（まね）きたいが、むさくるしい所（ところ）で<u>気が引ける</u>。

I'd like to invite my colleagues to my home, but it's such a shabby place
that I feel uncomfortable about it.

ki ga ii　気がいい　be kind; be generous

あの大工（だいく）さんは<u>気がいい</u>ので、ちょっとしたことは只（ただ）で直（なお）してく
れる。

That carpenter is generous, so s/he fixes little problems for free.

ki ga kawaru　気が変わる　change one's mind

休みに海に行く計画であったが、気が変わって、山へ行くことに
した。

I had planned to go to the beach for a vacation, but I changed my mind
and decided to go to the mountains.

ki ga ki de nai　気が気でない　be very concerned; be quite worried

あと五分で新幹線が出るというのに彼はまだ現れず、気が気でない。

Although the bullet train is going to leave in five minutes, he hasn't
shown up yet and I am terribly worried.

ki ga kiku　気が利く

(1) be considerate; attentive

今度のお手伝いさんは気が利かない人で言われたことしかしない。

Our new maid is a person with no initiative, and s/he only does the things
s/he is told to do.

(2) chic; fashionable; trendy

隣のおばさんは旅行のおみやげにいつも気の利いたものを買って
来てくれる。

On her travels, the lady next door always buys trendy souvenirs for me.

彼女はそんなに高いものを着ているわけではないが、スカーフの使い方が<u>気が利いている</u>ので素敵にみえる。

It's not that the things she wears are so expensive, but she wears scarves stylishly and so she looks great.

ki ga magireru　気が紛れる　be diverted from; be distracted from; be absorbed in

悲しい時には、運動をすると、<u>気が紛れる</u>。

When you are sad, if you do physical exercise, you will be distracted from your sadness.

ki ga mawaru　気が回る　be solicitous; be attentive

この宿の女将はよく<u>気が回る</u>人なので、初めての客もくつろげる。

The proprietress of this inn is a very solicitous person, so even first-time customers feel relaxed.

ki ga meiru　気が滅入る　become depressed; feel dispirited

今年は長梅雨で、くる日もくる日も雨ばかりで<u>気が滅入って</u>しまう。

This year the rainy season is long. It's been raining day after day and I feel depressed.

ki ga mijikai　気が短い　be short-tempered

うちの父は<u>気が短く</u>、ちょっとしたことにもすぐ怒り出す。

My father has a short temper—he gets angry over the slightest thing.

ki ga momeru 気が揉める be worried; be anxious; be concerned

娘の就職がなかなか決まらず、気が揉める。

My daughter hasn't found a job, and I am concerned.

ki ga muku 気が向く be interested in

足の向くまま、気の向くままに旅に出た。

I went on a trip where my feet and inclination led me.

ki ga nagai 気が長い be patient

彼は気の長い人だから後三年ぐらい待つのは何てことない。

It's nothing for him to wait another three years because he's a patient person.

ki ga nai 気がない have no inclination to; do not feel like

映画に行こうとさそってみたが、彼は気がないのか、生返事しかしない。

I tried inviting him to go to a movie, but he gave only a noncommittal reply, so I guess he's not interested.

ki ga noru 気が乗る be interested in

役者は、気が乗らなくても、気が乗っているような顔をして演じなければならない。

Actors must pretend interest in their performance, even if they are not interested.

254

ki ga nukeru　気が抜ける　feel let down; lose interest in

試験だと思って準備して行ったのに、延期されて<u>気が抜けた</u>。

I thought there was going to be an exam, so I went prepared, but the exam was postponed and I felt let down.

ki ga omoi　気が重い　be dispirited; be morose; be depressed

あと一週間で期末試験が始まるかと思うと<u>気が重い</u>。

Whenever I think of finals beginning in a week, I get the blues.

ki ga ōi　気が多い　be changeable; be fickle; be capricious

あの学生は<u>気が多い</u>のか、いろいろな言語に手をつけるが、一つもものにならない。

I wonder whether that student isn't capricious. S/He tries her/his hand at many languages but hasn't mastered any of them.

ki ga ōkii　気が大きい　be generous; be bighearted

兄は酒を飲むと<u>気が大きく</u>なって大盤振舞いをする。

When my older brother drinks, he becomes bighearted and treats everyone.

ki ga seku　気がせく　feel rushed; feel pressed for time

原稿の締切りが近づいているのに、仕事がはかどらず、<u>気がせく</u>。

Although the deadline is approaching, my work is not progressing, and I feel pressed for time.

ki ga shirenai　気が知れない be incomprehensible

あんなにやさしい両親がありながら、家出してしまうとは、あの子の気が知れない。

I can't understand that child's leaving home despite having such kind parents.

ki ga shizumu　気が沈む be depressed

幼くして死なせてしまった息子のことを思うと気が沈む。

When I think about my son who died young, I get depressed.

ki ga sumu　気が済む be relieved; be satisfied; be at ease; be relaxed

清潔好きな人は毎日掃除をしないと気が済まない。

People who like things to be clean can't rest unless they clean every day.

ki ga suru　気がする have a feeling that

夕焼けの色から判断すると、明日は雨が降るような気がする。

Judging from the color of the sunset, I have a feeling that it will rain tomorrow.

ki ga susumanai　気が進まない be unwilling to; be reluctant to; hesitate to

気が進まない相手との結婚はしない方がいい。

You shouldn't marry someone you don't feel like marrying.

256

ki ga tatsu　気が立つ

(1) be irritable

入試前夜の学生は<u>気が立っている</u>から、そっとしておいてやるの
がよい。

Students are irritable on the eve of the entrance exams, so it is better just
to leave them alone.

(2) be high strung; be in shock; be jittery: be tense

明朝六時の飛行機で日本へ発つ。飛行機に遅れまいと<u>気が立って</u>
<u>いる</u>のか、なかなか眠れない。

I leave for Japan tomorrow on a 6:00 A.M. flight. I wonder if it's fear of
missing the plane, but I simply can't get to sleep.

ki ga togameru　気が咎める　feel guilty

病気で仕事を休んだのに、少し気分がよくなったからと言って、
夕方遊びに出かけるのは<u>気が咎める</u>。

I took the day off from work because I was sick, but I'm feeling better
now. So, I feel guilty about going out this evening.

257

ki ga tōku naru 気が遠くなる

(1) faint; lose consciousness

シャーロックホームズは暗やみの中で後ろから頭を殴られ気が遠くなった。

Sherlock Holmes was hit on the head from behind in the dark and lost consciousness.

(2) be unimaginable; be farfetched

五十年前には気の遠くなるような話に思われたインターネットが、今は現実となっている。

The Internet, considered a farfetched idea fifty years ago, has become a reality.

ki ga tsuku 気が付く notice

話が弾んで、気が付いたらもう真夜中であった。

We talked and talked, and when I noticed the time, it was already the middle of the night.

ki ga tsumaru 気が詰まる feel intimidated; be overwhelmed

あの先生は気難しくてそばにいると気が詰まるから、パーティーに呼ぶのはやめよう。

That teacher is hard to please, and when you're near him/her you feel intimidated, so let's not invite him/her to the party.

ki ga tsuyoi 気が強い be strong-willed; be strong-minded

うちのチビ<ruby>犬<rt>いぬ</rt></ruby>は<u>気が強くて</u>、<ruby>大<rt>おお</rt></ruby>きな犬にも<ruby>吠<rt>ほ</rt></ruby>えかかる。

My little dog is fearless and even barks at big dogs.

ki ga wakai 気が若い be young at heart

うちの<ruby>祖父<rt>そふ</rt></ruby>は<u>気が若くて</u>、<ruby>孫<rt>まご</rt></ruby>の<ruby>友達<rt>ともだち</rt></ruby>と<ruby>話<rt>はなし</rt></ruby>をするのが<ruby>好<rt>す</rt></ruby>きだ。

My grandfather is young at heart, and he likes to talk with his grandchildren's friends.

ki ga yasumaru 気が休まる be at peace; feel relaxed

<ruby>外<rt>そと</rt></ruby>に<ruby>出<rt>で</rt></ruby>て<ruby>木々<rt>きぎ</rt></ruby>の<ruby>梢<rt>こずえ</rt></ruby>から<ruby>聞<rt>き</rt></ruby>こえてくる<ruby>鳥<rt>とり</rt></ruby>の<ruby>声<rt>こえ</rt></ruby>を聞いていると、<u>気が休まる</u>。

When I go out and listen to the birds chirping in the treetops, I feel at peace.

ki ga yoi 気がよい See **ki ga ii**

ki ga yowai 気が弱い be spineless; be weak-willed; be timid; be softhearted

あの人は<u>気が弱くて</u><ruby>頼<rt>たの</rt></ruby>まれると<ruby>断<rt>ことわ</rt></ruby>り<ruby>切<rt>き</rt></ruby>れない。

That person is softhearted and can't refuse a request.

ki ga yowaru 気が弱る become dispirited

人は<ruby>健康<rt>けんこう</rt></ruby>を<ruby>害<rt>がい</rt></ruby>すると<u>気も弱る</u>ものである。

People become dispirited when their health suffers.

ki ga yurumu　気が緩む　be relaxed

おおしごと　おわ　　とたん　　　　　　　　　　　　　　　　　　　つか　で
大仕事が終った途端に、気が緩んでどっと疲れが出た。

The moment the big job was finished, I became relaxed and then all of a sudden felt extremely tired.

ki ni iru　気に入る　like; be satisfied with

かれ　あたま　　　　　　　　　　　　　こうまん　はな　　　　　　　　　い
彼は頭のいい男だが、高慢な話しっぷりが気に入らない。

He is quite intelligent, but I don't like his arrogant style of speech.

ki ni kakaru　気に掛かる　weigh on one's mind

ゆう　いや　ゆめ　　　　　　　　　　　　　　　しごと　て
夕べ嫌な夢を見たのが気に掛かって、仕事も手につかない。

The nightmare I had last night is weighing on my mind, and I can't work.

ki ni kakeru 気に掛ける worry; weigh on one's mind

うわさ　　　　　　　　　　　　　　なに　でき
人の噂を気に掛けていては何も出来ない。

If you worry about rumors, you won't be able to do anything.

ki ni kanau　気に適う　be satisfied with; like

おや　　　　　　　　けっこんあいて　　　　　　　　　　かんたん
親の気に適う結婚相手を見つけるのはそう簡単ではない。

It is not that easy to find a marriage partner my parents will like.

ki ni kuwanai 気に食わない dislike; hate

この靴は形はいいのだが、どうも色が気に食わない。

I'm pleased with the style of this pair of shoes, but somehow I don't like the color.

ki ni naru 気になる weigh on one's mind

親はいつまでも子供のことが気になるものだ。

Parents will always worry about their children.

ki ni sawaru 気に障る get on (someone's) nerves

あの人は悪い人ではないが、いつも自分のうちの自慢話をするのが気に障る。

That person is not a bad person, but his/her constant boasting about his/her own family gets on my nerves.

ki ni somu 気に染む be satisfied with; like

仕事であれば、気に染まないことでもしなければならない。

As long as it's my job, I have to do it, even if it is something that I don't find pleasing.

ki ni suru 気にする mind; care; concern oneself with

人の悪口など気にする必要はない。

There's no need to pay any attention to malicious gossip (about you).

ki ni tomeru 気に留める give heed to; take notice of

彼女は友人の忠告を<u>気に留める</u>様子もない。

She doesn't show any sign of paying attention to her friends' advice.

ki ni yamu 気に病む worry about; feel bad about; take to heart

受験に失敗したからと言って<u>気に病む</u>ことはない。

You don't have to feel bad just because you failed the entrance exam.

ki no okenai 気の置けない feel at home; feel at ease

<u>気の置けない</u>人達とパーティーをするのは楽しい。

It's fun to have a party with people with whom you feel at ease.

ki o harasu 気を晴らす divert oneself; divert one's mind; relieve one's mind

一日中読書ばかりしているので<u>気を晴らす</u>ために泳ぎにでも行った方がいいかもしれない。

I've been reading all day, so maybe I should go swimming for a change.

ki o haru 気を張る be tense

そんなに<u>気を張っている</u>とすぐに疲れてしまうから、気を楽にする方がいい。

If you are so tense, you'll tire yourself out, so you ought to relax.

ki o hikitateru　気を引き立てる　cheer up; lift up one's spirits

夫の死後、悲しみに明けくれている友人の気を引き立てようと、
音楽会に誘ってみた。

Trying to cheer up my friend, who has been lost in sadness day in and
day out since her husband died, I invited her to a concert.

ki o hiku　気を引く　attract attention; arouse attention

口先だけで相手の気を引こうとしてもすぐに見破られてしまう。

If you are insincere in trying to attract another's attention, you'll be seen
through right away.

ki o ireru　気を入れる　work hard; be attentive

子供の時に気を入れてピアノの練習をすればよかったと後悔して
いる。

I wish that when I was a child I had worked hard at practicing the piano.

ki o kaeru　気を変える　change one's mind

今晩は映画に行かないでいようと思っていたが、気を変えて、誘
われるままに、行くことにした。

I'd been thinking that I wouldn't go to the movies tonight, but I changed
my mind and decided to go, just as I had been invited to.

ki o kikaseru 気を利かせる exercise tact; have good sense

私の友達が訪ねてくると、ルームメートは気を利かせて、すぐに
図書館へ行ってくれる。

When my friend comes over to visit, my roommate tactfully goes straight
off to the library.

ki o kubaru 気を配る be sensitive to

「いじめ」が社会問題となっている今日、教師は子供の心理状態
に常に気を配っていなければならない。

Nowadays, since bullying has become a societal problem, teachers must
be sensitive at all times to (school) children's psychological states.

ki o mawasu 気を回す be overly concerned

新居に移転するに当り、母は気を回して余計なものまで買ってく
れた。

When I moved to a new house, my mother made a fuss over it and even
bought me things I didn't need.

ki o momu 気を揉む worry about; be anxious about

株屋は株価の変動に毎日気を揉む。

Stockbrokers worry every day over the changes in stock prices.

ki o motasu 気を持たす encourage; invite

買う気もないのに、セールスマンに質問をして<u>気を持たす</u>のは罪なことである。

It is wrong for you to ask questions and invite expectations on the part of the salesperson when you have no intention of buying anything.

ki o otosu 気を落とす be disheartened; be dispirited

受験に失敗したくらいで、そんなに<u>気を落とす</u>ことはない。

If failing the entrance exam is all it is, then it's not something you should be so disheartened about.

ki o raku ni suru 気を楽にする take a load off one's mind; feel relieved

深呼吸をして<u>気を楽にする</u>と、気持が落ち着く。

When you breathe deeply and relax, you feel at ease.

ki o shizumeru 気を静める be calm

人前で話す時は、慌てないで<u>気を静めて</u>話すに限る。

When speaking in front of a group, all you have to do is stay calm and not get flustered.

ki o sosoru 気をそそる arouse one's interest in; be invited; be attracted

秋の夜、鈴虫の音に<u>気をそそられて</u>、散歩に出かけた。

Attracted by the chirping of crickets, I went out for a stroll one autumn evening.

ki o tsukau　気を使う　care about; worry about

妻の母は私に対して<u>気を使い</u>過ぎるので、訪ねるのが億劫である。

My wife's mother is too solicitous, so it is tiresome to go visit her.

ki o tsukeru　気を付ける　be careful

この辺は夜危ないので<u>気を付ける</u>に越したことはない。

It's dangerous around here at night, so you'd be best advised to take care.

ki o waruku suru　気を悪くする　become displeased

冗談が過ぎると<u>気を悪くする</u>こともある。

If you go too far with your jokes, there will be times when you make people feel bad.

ki o yasumeru　気を休める　take it easy; feel relaxed; take a break

この会社の秘書は、次から次に訪問客の質問にのってやって、<u>気を休める</u>暇もない。

Secretaries in this company never get any rest because they are so involved in answering visitors' questions one after another.

ki o yoku suru　気をよくする　feel good about; be pleased

褒められて<u>気をよくしている</u>と、おだてられているに過ぎないことがある。

When you are feeling good about being praised, sometimes it turns out to have been nothing but flattery.

266

ki o yurumeru 気を緩める relax one's attention; take it easy

ロッククライマーは、登^{のぼ}る時^{とき}よりも下^おりる時にこそ<u>気を緩める</u>な
という。

Rock climbers say that, even more than on the way up, it's on the way
down that you should not relax your attention.

ki o yurusu 気を許す trust; relax one's guard

旅行中^{りょこうちゅう}は親切^{しんせつ}そうな人にうっかり<u>気を許して</u>ひどい目^めにあうこと
があるかもしれないから気を付^つけた方^{ほう}がいい。

When you are traveling, you're apt to run into trouble if you let down
your guard with someone who looks kind, so you had better be careful.

Appendix B

mi ga hairu 身が入る be interested in; be absorbed in; be engrossed in

彼女は仕事に<u>身が入って</u>いないから、いつも失敗ばかりしている。

She is not interested in her work, so she's always making mistakes.

mi ga iru 身が入る See **mi ga hairu**

mi ga karui 身が軽い have few responsibilities

父は長年勤めていた会社を定年で退職してから<u>身が軽く</u>なったのか、いつもフラリと旅に出て行く。

My father seems to feel so liberated after retiring from the company where he worked for so long that he's always going off on trips unexpectedly.

mi ni amaru　身に余る　be more than one deserves

<ruby>社会福祉貢献<rt>しゃかいふくしこうけん</rt></ruby>への<ruby>功績<rt>こうせき</rt></ruby>が<ruby>認<rt>みと</rt></ruby>められ、<ruby>天皇陛下<rt>てんのうへいか</rt></ruby>にじきじきのねぎらいの<ruby>言葉<rt>ことば</rt></ruby>をいただき身に余る<ruby>光栄<rt>こうえい</rt></ruby>であった。

My contribution to social welfare services was recognized, and I received words of appreciation directly from His Majesty the Emperor. I felt undeserving of the honor.

mi ni au　身に合う　be suitable; be balanced

身に合わない<ruby>結婚<rt>けっこん</rt></ruby>は<ruby>不幸<rt>ふこう</rt></ruby>のもとである。

An unsuitable marriage is the cause of unhappiness.

mi ni naru　身になる

(1)　become one's own

<ruby>長<rt>なが</rt></ruby>い<ruby>間<rt>あいだ</rt></ruby>中国語を勉強しているのに、身になっていないのか、中国に行った<ruby>時<rt>とき</rt></ruby><ruby>上手<rt>じょうず</rt></ruby>に話せなかった。

Although I have been studying Chinese for a long time, I guess I haven't acquired it, because I couldn't say anything clever when I went to China.

(2)　put oneself in another's place/shoes

<ruby>子供<rt>こども</rt></ruby>の身になって<ruby>考<rt>かんが</rt></ruby>えると、<ruby>厳<rt>きび</rt></ruby>しい<ruby>親<rt>おや</rt></ruby>よりも<ruby>甘<rt>あま</rt></ruby>い親の<ruby>方<rt>ほう</rt></ruby>がいいのだろう。

If you put yourself in a child's shoes, then it's probably better to have softhearted parents than strict ones.

269

mi ni oboe ga aru　身に覚えがある　know by personal experience

盗みをはたらいたと責められたが、私には全く<u>身に覚えのない</u>ことであった。

I was accused of stealing, but I knew nothing about it.

mi ni shimiru　身に染みる　feel keenly; appreciate fully

落ちぶれて頼る人もなく途方にくれていた時に、身も知らぬ隣人に手を差し伸べられ、その親切を<u>身に染みて</u>感じた。

When I was down and out, at a loss with no one to rely on, a neighbor whom I didn't know at all gave me a helping hand, and I was deeply touched by his/her kindness.

mi ni tsuku　身に付く　acquire; become one's own

彼は子供の頃しつけられたテーブルマナーが<u>身に付いている</u>ので、どこに出しても恥ずかしくない。

Since he acquired proper table manners as a child, he won't be an embarrassment no matter where you may take him.

mi ni tsumasareru　身につまされる　sympathize deeply with; feel deeply for

戦後住むところも食べるものもなく苦労した人々の話を聞くと<u>身につまされる</u>。

When I hear stories about people after the war who had no place to live and nothing to eat, I sympathize deeply with them.

mi o ayamaru 身をあやまる go astray; succumb to temptation

<ruby>若<rt>わか</rt></ruby>い<ruby>時<rt>とき</rt></ruby>に<ruby>酒<rt>さけ</rt></ruby>で<u>身をあやまり</u>、<ruby>会社<rt>かいしゃ</rt></ruby>もクビになってしまった。

When I was young, I went astray on account of liquor, and (among other things) I ended up being fired from my job.

mi o hiku 身を引く resign one's post; give up

<ruby>離婚後<rt>りこんご</rt></ruby><ruby>子供<rt>こども</rt></ruby>を<ruby>引<rt>ひ</rt></ruby>き<ruby>取<rt>と</rt></ruby>りたいと思ったが、<ruby>子供<rt>こども</rt></ruby>の<ruby>教育<rt>きょういく</rt></ruby>を<ruby>考<rt>かんが</rt></ruby>えて<u>身を引く</u>ことにした。

After the divorce, I wanted to get custody of my children, but, thinking about their education, I decided to give up.

mi o horobosu 身をほろぼす ruin oneself

<ruby>彼<rt>かれ</rt></ruby>は<ruby>会社<rt>かいしゃ</rt></ruby>を<ruby>解雇<rt>かいこ</rt></ruby>されてから<ruby>酒<rt>さけ</rt></ruby>におぼれるようになり、<u>身をほろぼしてしまった</u>。

After being fired, he reached the point where he drowned himself in sake and went to ruin.

mi o ireru 身を入れる devote oneself to; take an active interest in; exert oneself

<ruby>外国語<rt>がいこくご</rt></ruby>は<u>身を入れて</u>しないと<ruby>上手<rt>じょうず</rt></ruby>になるものではない。

A foreign language is something that you won't become good at unless you devote yourself to it.

mi o kakusu 身を隠す hide oneself; conceal oneself

彼は急に有名になり何処に行ってもレポーターにとりまかれるので、しばらく身を隠すよりほかはない。

He has become famous all of a sudden. No matter where he goes, he is surrounded by reporters, so there's nothing for him to do but to keep out of sight for a while.

mi o katameru 身を固める

(1) marry and settle down

もう三十を過ぎたので、そろそろ身を固めてはどうかと、近くの人がお見合いの写真をもって来た。

Since I'm already over thirty, people in the neighborhood have brought around photos of potential marital partners, suggesting that I should get married and settle down one of these days.

(2) be attired in; wear

新入生は制服に身を固めて入学式に臨んだ。

The new students attended the entrance ceremony dressed in their school uniforms.

mi o kezuru 身を削る suffer a hardship

いくら親友だからと言って、自分の身を削ってまで面倒をみる
必要はない。

There's no need to look after a friend to the point of suffering yourself,
no matter how close a friend s/he may be.

mi o kirareru 身を切られる

(1) be harrowing, distressing

大火事で家屋をなくした人々は、身を切られるような思いで一夜
を過ごした。

People who lost their houses in the big fire spent the night in great
distress.

(2) be piercing, chilling, penetrating

大火事で家屋をなくした人々は、身を切られるような寒さの中で
一夜を過ごした。

People who lost their houses in the big fire spent the night in the
piercing cold.

mi o ko ni suru 身を粉にする work hard; work to the bone

十九世紀にアメリカに移民して来た多くの人々は身を粉にして働
き財産を築き上げた。

Many people who immigrated to America in the nineteenth century
managed to build up some capital by working themselves to the bone.

273

mi o korosu　身を殺す　perform a benevolent act; sacrifice oneself

身を殺して不幸な人々のために働くなど、わがままな私にできる
わけがない。

I'm too selfish to do such a thing as sacrifice myself for people who are
less fortunate.

mi o makaseru　身を任せる　give oneself up to

おぼれかけている時は、あがこうとせず救助の人に身を任せる方
がよい。

If you are drowning, don't struggle, but surrender yourself to the people
who are trying to rescue you.

何事においても努力は必要であるが、時の運に身を任せる方がよ
い場合もある。

Effort is essential in everything, but there are times when it's better that
you entrust yourself to fate.

mi o nageru　身を投げる　throw oneself into (a river, the ocean, etc.)

不景気を反映して海に身を投げて自殺する人が増えてきている。

In reaction to the weak economy, the number of people who commit
suicide by throwing themselves into the sea is increasing.

mi o okosu　身を起こす　rise up; make one's way up the social ladder

豊臣秀吉は一介の足軽から身を起こしたことで知られている。

Toyotomi Hideyoshi is known to have risen from (the position of) a simple foot soldier.

mi o otosu　身を落とす　degrade oneself; demean oneself

彼女はあれほど前途を期待されていた人であったのに、乞食に身を落としていると聞いて我が耳を疑った。

Although great things were expected of her, I heard that she had descended to the level of a beggar, and I didn't believe my ears.

mi o tateru　身を立てる　establish oneself; rise in the world

演劇で身を立てようとニューヨークにやって来たが、なかなか思うようにいかない。

I came to New York to establish myself on the stage, but it isn't going as I'd like it to.

mi o yatsusu　身をやつす　disguise oneself

水戸黄門は老隠居に身をやつして旅に出たと言われている。

Mito Kōmon is said to have gone on trips disguised as an elderly gentleman in retirement.

275

mi o yoseru　身を寄せる　stay with; find shelter with

阪神大震災で家をなくし、しばらく親戚の家に身を寄せていた。
We lost our house in the Great Kobe Earthquake, and we stayed with relatives for a while.